Careers in Politics for the New Woman

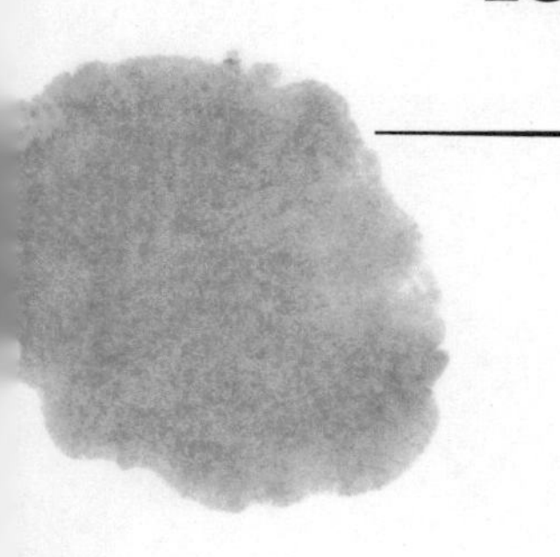

Careers in Politics
for the New Woman

by Alice Lynn Booth

CHOOSING CAREERS
AND LIFE-STYLES

Franklin Watts/New York/London/1978

To Harry and Sylvia Booth with love

Photographs courtesy of:

United Press International: pp. 2, 6, 28, 31, 42 (bottom), 80, 84, 87, 101, 109;
Mount Vernon College, The Washington Institute for Women in Politics: pp. 15 (top), 18 (top), 42 (top);
State of New York, Office of the Lieutenant Governor: p. 15 (bottom);
Rutgers University, Center for the American Woman and Politics: p. 18 (bottom);
Civil Service Employees' Association: p. 51 (top);
International Ladies' Garment Workers' Union—"Justice": p. 51 (bottom);
Bella Abzug for Mayor Headquarters: pp. 64, 96;
Bellamy Campaign Committee: p. 89.

Library of Congress Cataloging in Publication Data

Booth, Alice Lynn.
    Careers in politics for the new woman.

    (Choosing careers and life-styles)
    Bibliography: p.
    Includes index.
    SUMMARY: Politically-active women discuss their
careers as lobbyists, elected officials, and campaign
workers.
    1. Women in politics—United States—Juvenile litera-
ture. 2. Politics, Practical—Vocational guidance—
Juvenile literature. [1. Politics, Practical—Vocational
guidance. 2. Vocational guidance. 3. Women in politics]
I. Title.
HQ1391.U5B66   329′.0023   77-5104
ISBN 0-531-01313-8

Acknowledgments

I want to express my affectionate thanks to friends who spirited me through this work, particularly Peggy Sange, Harvey Walters, Joan Tapper, Esther Geil, Karan Dement, Dick D'Amato, and Barbara J. Katz. My special gratitude goes to the women in this book who gave me their time and their encouragement because they believed in the project. I am especially grateful to Betsey Wright of the National Women's Education Fund whose assistance and guidance eased my task from beginning to end.

Contents

Careers in Politics for the New Woman

The excitement of politics is evident as delegates,
party workers, and supporters of Jimmy Carter rejoice following his
nomination as the Democratic presidential candidate in 1976.

1

Why Politics?

There are two good reasons for women to consider politics as a career. First, if women want to make our country a better place to live, choosing politics as a career is the most direct route toward helping to make that happen. And since women make up more than half of the country's population, they should have an equal say in determining its policies.

The second reason has to do with you as an individual. Few other careers you might choose will prove as exciting, as varied, or as challenging. Politics needs people who are bright and talented and who have new ideas. If you want to use your mind and develop your intellectual potential, politics offers that opportunity.

Until recently, politics was an exclusively male club in the United States. The talk, the men said, was too rough and the rules too tough for "ladies." But that was just an excuse the men gave to keep the women out. From the example set by the new political women, it has become apparent that a woman can also be "tough" if that means standing up for what she believes. She is not afraid of conflict. She can fight hard and she can take defeat. She understands how to negotiate without selling out. The voters know it. Only the old political players are still trying to keep women out.

Is politics right for you? It won't make you rich. It can make you famous. It can also be exhausting, time consuming, and frustrating. If you cherish time at home and love your privacy, politics will probably not suit you. If intimate personal relationships are as important to you as hard and creative work, then politics will force you to sacrifice something important.

You must enjoy pressure. You have to like people. You cannot buckle under criticism. If you are committed to your beliefs, you can expect to be attacked. If you are not, you do not belong in politics.

One reward of politics is power—the power to implement your beliefs. The new political woman is not shy about liking power. She considers it an opportunity and a responsibility, not something to take lightly and certainly not something to abuse. Power is the means to a better and fairer government. For women today, power is also a vehicle for achieving social change, including sexual equality. No matter whether you run for office or seek a professional job, and whatever your political goals, by choosing politics as a career you can help to see to it that those goals are achieved.

2

The Changing Role of Women in Politics

When four feminist luminaries, Congresswoman Bella Abzug, Betty Friedan, Gloria Steinem, and Fannie Lou Hamer, announced the formation of the National Women's Political Caucus (NWPC) in 1971, they knew that if the women's movement was to mature, the women of America would have to seek political power. "We want to take our rightful position as 50 percent of every elected and appointed body in this country," said Gloria Steinem. "No one gives political power. It must be taken and we will take it." Picketing the Miss America Pageant might make headlines, but it wouldn't get the Equal Rights Amendment enacted, make credit available to women, give women equal pay for equal work, create equal opportunities in education, or set up child-care centers.

The multi-partisan NWPC called for equal representation of the sexes in all government bodies and at the nominating conventions. They proposed a campaign to thrust women into political power at all levels of government. They offered support to candidates, male and female, who would speak for women's interests.

That may not sound like the war cry of a revolutionary movement but it was. Fifty years after winning the right to vote, women were still political outsiders. It had taken 70 years of struggle on the part of organized suffragette groups—women

Four of the main speakers at the opening of the National
Women's Political Caucus: (left to right) Betty Smith,
former Wisconsin Republican Party chairperson, Dorothy Haener
of the United Automobile Workers' Union, Fannie Lou Hamer,
and Gloria Steinem.

who leafleted, lectured, lobbied, picketed, and went to jail—to get the right to vote in 1920. Rather than enter the political fray, the suffragettes formed the League of Women Voters, which attempted to reform government from the outside. The League has abstained from partisan activity and has never sought political power for women. Some women did join the parties, but they became foot soldiers for the campaigns of men, never aspiring to public office or being consulted on policy-making.

Even now, women constitute a tiny minority in the decision-making bodies of the nation, from school board to Congress. For example, although women make up 54 percent of the voting population and more than 40 percent of the labor force, there were no women in the U.S. Senate in 1977 and less than 4 percent of the House seats were held by women. And the Center for the American Woman and Politics at Rutgers University says women held only 4 to 7 percent of the nation's public offices in 1976.

Yet we do have substantial evidence of recent progress for women in politics. In 1968, for instance, only 13 percent of the delegates to the Democratic National Convention and 17 percent of Republican delegates were women, while in 1976, the figures were 33 and 31 percent respectively. Women are beginning to participate in many new and important ways. In 1974, we elected a woman governor who had, for the first time, not followed her husband into office. Ella Grasso of Connecticut had spent more than 20 years working her way up through the political ranks. She won an office that even she hadn't believed available to a woman.

That same year, New York State Senator Mary Anne Krupsak fought against her party's leaders to get the Democratic nomination for lieutenant governor. And when it was up to the voters, she was elected, and became the first woman to hold that position in her state.

It was also the year when Janet Gray Hayes, a mother of four children, campaigned through a primary against six other candidates, a run-off, and a general election, to become the first woman mayor of a large city—San Jose, California. Hayes had become involved in politics after trying for two years to get a crossing guard at her children's school. She had become "totally disillusioned with the workings of local government," she says.

The Hayes victory gave Lila Cockrell, vice-mayor of San Antonio, Texas, the courage she needed to seek the mayor's office. She had been told in 1970 that she would make a great mayor if only she were a man. In 1975, Lila won that title in the nation's largest city that is governed by a woman.

There has been a slow, steady increase in the numbers of women running and winning election to office. In 1976, more women ran for office than ever before and the number of women in state legislatures increased by 10 percent. Dixie Lee Ray was elected Governor of Washington, the second woman elected in her own right to the top state office. However, women were unable to break up the all-male hegemony of the U.S. Senate, and one less woman serves in the House of Representatives in 1977 than served in 1976.

By far, 1974 was the year of dramatic victories for women. The number of women in state legislatures increased that year by 26 percent. Also that year Elaine Noble, a lesbian, was elected to the Massachusetts legislature, the first avowed homosexual to win such an office.

President Gerald Ford named 60-year-old Mary Louise Smith to chair the Republican party in 1974, the first time a woman was picked for that spot. At the Democratic Mini-Convention in the same year, women startled leaders by demonstrating better organization than any group there. By the 1976 Democratic Convention, women were a political force.

A poll taken in September 1975 by George Gallup showed seven out of ten Americans saying that the nation would be governed as well or better if more women held public office. Among the principal reasons given, according to Gallup, were that women are more conscientious and economy minded. The survey showed a record proportion of Americans—73 percent —ready to vote for a woman as president.

When Cathy Riley ran for the Maryland General Assembly in 1974, she discovered a change in voters' attitudes toward women. "People were disgusted with the political system and wanted to try something new," she says. "In 1970, people opposed me because I was a woman. But in 1974, some people voted for me on that basis alone." Cathy had spent two years working as a legislative assistant in the Maryland legislature and then went on to defeat one of her bosses at the polls.

Women have learned to do more than run for office. They have lobbied for women's issues, organized task forces within the parties, set up caucuses around the nation, and demanded promises from candidates.

Women have emerged as professionals, working as campaign managers and technicians, as lobbyists and political organizers, as legislative and administrative assistants to public officials. They have asked for and received proper titles and salaries. In fact, more women held professional positions in the 1976 campaigns than ever before. Their power was limited and their numbers few, but for the first time male candidates saw the need for women other than typists and receptionists in staff positions.

But what is most significant is the change in women's attitudes about themselves. Women are gaining the confidence and skills to demand an equal role in political life. And through powerful organizations, they are helping one another achieve that equality.

Women have learned not to be afraid to be themselves. They know that they can be tough, assertive, competent, and successful and still remain women. And because women have been socialized differently from men, they can bring a new perspective to politics. "The woman's view is more personal and human," says NWPC Executive Director, Jane McMichael. "Women can bring government back to a personal level where it touches people."

Betsey Wright went to Washington in 1973 to organize the Women's Education Fund, NWPC's education arm. She has traveled around the country teaching women how to organize political campaigns and run for office. "Every time a woman runs," Betsey says, "she clarifies the role of women in politics and makes it easier for the next woman. The women running today are more sophisticated than they were two years ago.

They have organized better campaigns. They know how to work with the press and get skilled workers. They are stronger candidates. The obstacles women face are still there, but our ability to deal with them has improved enormously."

Betsey says the true test of the women's movement is how women perceive one another, that is, to what extent women themselves believe in their fellow women's competence in office. And she has been heartened by the growing percentage of women who give equal consideration to a woman candidate. Without the women's cooperation among themselves, her labors would be fruitless. "We must support one another if we're ever to have numbers of women entering politics," she has said. "There are plenty of women who are motivated. We have to give them the confidence and support to do it. It has to happen at the local level. Women must care passionately enough to build the organizational bases for campaigns."

Once in office, women are continuing to help one another. "The main difference between today and 17 years ago is that women are much more conscious of helping one another," says Connecticut's Secretary of State Gloria Schaffer. "When Ella ran for governor, some political friends warned me not to support her. They said she'd have to get rid of me. I don't think either Ella or I ever thought of that. The old line 'pols' still think that way about women. But the voters are way beyond that."

Two years after Janet Gray Hayes was elected to the city council of San Jose, she sought out another woman and helped her win election to it. "We must work our way out of this Dick and Jane society," says Hayes, who never leaves a post without making sure at least one other woman follows her into it.

A support network of professional political women has also developed. "Ten years ago that didn't exist," says Susan Tannenbaum, director of Connecticut's Washington office. "Finding a job was a nightmare. Today, women are helping one another. Those who have been through it want to make it easier for others." The woman of today can plot a political career. Her older sisters have broken ground.

Another great change is that women of all ages and life-styles are pursuing political careers. A few years ago, the only woman who ran for office was married and had grown children. Today, single and divorced women and mothers with young children are winning elections. Pat Schroeder campaigned for the U.S. Congress in 1972 when her son was in nursery school and her daughter in diapers. Pat's husband, an attorney with political ambitions, had decided that Pat would be the stronger candidate. Congresswoman Yvonne Burke, a divorcée, remarried during her first term and became the first member of Congress to have a baby while in office.

The new political woman views politics as a profession rather than an extension of volunteer community service. She's beginning at the lower levels of politics, and building a political base and experience equal to her male counterpart. Women are running for offices that were in the past reserved for men, and are achieving professional positions previously held only by men. The new woman is broadening the image of the political woman, opening up opportunities that promise far greater future participation.

Women embarking on a political career still face more obstacles than men. Women candidates have far greater difficulty raising money than men. Jobs are harder to come by for women. Women must be better prepared and work harder than men for an equal shot. The promise of tomorrow is that women today can prepare themselves for a political career, and with dedication and determination, have a reasonable hope of succeeding. Ten years ago, few women entered politics because they lacked the vision that opportunity provides. Today the opportunity is real. If you have the vision, then it's up to you to grab the opportunity.

3

Preparing for a Political Career

Politics is the only profession with almost no formal requirements. To run for office, you have only to be a citizen, a registered voter, and of a certain age and have lived in one area for a certain length of time. Age and residency requirements vary with the office. Even the presidency has no other minimum requirements.

The way to become a political professional is nearly as ill defined. If your best friend winds up in the White House, you could become the president's chief of staff or a cabinet officer. Just as in running for office, there are no special qualifications needed for employment on Capitol Hill or on the White House staff.

In the old days of patronage politics, the political boss controlled *all* government jobs and doled them out to relatives, friends, campaign workers, and contributors. That is how political machines kept themselves in power. Today the civil service system has ended that. Only the elected official's personal staff remains a vestige of the old system. If your father or mother is a big campaign contributor, your chances for a job may be greatly enhanced. In too many cases, it's often whom you know rather than what you know that gets you the job.

In the past, a woman's access to political positions was so limited that her qualifications didn't matter. The question most frequently asked was, "Can you type?" Her education and degrees were irrelevant. Today most public officials say they are seeking qualified women for professional slots. Unfortunately, it's difficult to define just what it means to be qualified.

In Anne Arundel County, Maryland, one highly placed official gave this explanation for not placing a woman in a certain high administrative job: "It's a tough job. It requires someone who can work nights and women don't want to do that." And despite statements by County Executive Robert Pascal that he wanted to hire women for professional jobs, he only explained their absence by saying, "I couldn't find any."

California's youthful governor Edmund G. "Jerry" Brown, Jr., put two women on his seven-person cabinet, the first women cabinet members in California history. Later, he made Rose Elizabeth Bird, his agriculture secretary, the first woman member and Chief Justice of California's Supreme Court. Brown hired women to head the Department of Veteran Affairs and the Parole Board, unusual roles for women. Governor Brown told me he had no difficulty finding "qualified, capable" women, and it was "time women were included in government."

But not many public officials seek women out. Opportunities are limited and politics is a competitive field. For a woman to succeed, she must be better than her male competition. She has to work harder, assert herself more, and have better credentials to have an equal chance.

How best to prepare yourself for a political career is a difficult question. Trying to work your way up from the typing pool, a ladder males never climb, may get you stuck on rung one. (Knowing *how* to type is an asset for any professional, of course.)

Probably the best approach is to aim high. The woman who applies for the job of legislative assistant and accepts one answering mail is going to do the job she accepts. It's wiser to hold out for the more responsible position, even if it means being unemployed for a while.

Presenting yourself as a professional, however, doesn't mean stepping into the field with a high school diploma and a knowledge of politics based on a high school civics course. It means carefully plotting out the avenues to success and getting the process under way as early as you can.

There are two aspects of preparing yourself for a career in politics. Whether you aspire to be president or the president's chief adviser, you should engage in both. One is getting the formal education—earning a degree, preferably graduate, in political science, economics, public affairs, or public administration, or graduating from law school. The other is serving as apprentice—working in campaigns; joining the Young Republicans or Young Democrats, the League of Women Voters, the National Women's Political Caucus; running for delegate to your party's national convention; becoming a party worker.

And you need not wait to finish your education before beginning your apprenticeship. Even as a high school student, you might explore the possibility of assisting a local government official or working on a special community project of your own. For college students, numerous internship programs, which send you into the inner circuits of government—local, state, and federal—are available. In Washington, Congress, the White House, and the federal agencies, as well as political parties, public interest groups, and women's organizations, have internship programs. Most state legislatures have programs with local colleges, which may offer either the chance to earn credit toward your degree or a small salary.

Working as an intern gives you a head start. Many women in professional positions in Washington began as college interns. An intern can find out whether she likes politics and is good at it. She will meet people who can be helpful later on. As an intern, you will have the opportunity to learn how the whole process works. Some interns complain they get only drudge work to do, but even then, they learn a lot simply through exposure.

"I worked in the pressroom of the Democratic National Committee one summer while in college," says Esther Newberg, whose résumé includes professional positions with Senator Robert F. Kennedy, Abraham Ribicoff, Congresswoman Bella Abzug, and the New York State Democratic Committee. "I did anything anyone told me to do. Essentially, I went for coffee

**Mount Vernon College student Janis Shipe interned with
Jeanne M. Holm, special assistant to the president for
women's affairs.**

**Paula Ziverdling (left), a college student interning in
the office of New York's Lieutenant Governor Mary Anne Krupsak,
works with staff researcher Anna McIntosh.**

and did secretarial work. If you're bright, they see it right away. You have to be prepared to listen and stuff envelopes and do a lot of rotten things. But if you don't understand the process from the bottom looking up, you'll never understand it from the top looking down."

Her internship at the committee turned into a full-time job when she graduated. At that point, Esther "forgot how to type. I insisted on getting paid and having responsibility," she says.

Competition for a summer internship in Congress or the White House is stiff. You have to apply for one through the White House Director for Youth Affairs or your congressmember. White House interns earn the equivalent of a GS-4 or GS-5 salary (the low rung of civil service). Congressmembers each get $1,000 a summer to hire interns. And this they usually divide among two or three students.

But those aren't the only internships available—even in Washington. The National Center for Public Service Internship Programs publishes a directory describing undergraduate and graduate Washington internships for students. It's available for $6.00 by writing NCPSI, 1735 Eye Street, N.W., Suite 601, Washington, D.C. 20006.

One of these programs is run by the Washington Center for Learning Alternatives. The center works with colleges to bring students to Washington for a semester. WCLA provides housing, seminars, and educational programs that tie in with the internship experience, and students receive college credit. In 1975, 62 percent of the participants were women. For information, write Mr. Bill Burke, WCLA, 1705 DeSales Street, N.W., Washington, D.C. 20036.

For Jill Schuker, who is now executive director of the New England Congressional Caucus, the summer spent as a college intern in Senator Robert F. Kennedy's office launched her political career.

"It gave me an interest in politics that took me beyond the mental gymnastics of school into practicalities," Jill says. "There was involvement with issues that were important to me, such as civil rights. You got the feeling that positive things could be accomplished. Once, when a staff member left, I spent three weeks in the press office. Senator Kennedy was very accessible. I researched his first newsletter. He set up meetings for us with political figures. There was excitement in the air. Friendships I made there were important contacts later on. When Senator Kennedy announced his intention to seek the presidency, Joe Dolan, his administrative assistant, called and asked me if I would like to work in the campaign."

There isn't any one best education to prepare yourself for a political career. Most of today's career women in politics have a degree in political science, but nearly all wonder about its practical value. "I think political science is a useless major," says Anne Canby, director of the campaign consulting project of the National Committee for an Effective Congress. She worked for Congressman Paul McCloskey for several years before taking her current job. "My politics," she says, "were learned on the ground."

Essentially, Anne is correct. Most political science courses deal only with theory. The training that is essential to a political career is better received by working in a campaign or as an intern.

But some colleges do offer classes in applied politics, which can be useful. Moreover, there is also a movement under way of women political scientists to offer more practical courses emphasizing the role of women in politics. For example, in 1974, Mount Vernon College in Washington, D.C., opened its Washington Institute in Politics. The director is Susan Tolchin, a political scientist and coauthor with her journalist husband, Martin, of the book *Clout—Womanpower and Politics*. Students enrolled in a degree program in public affairs and government can study campaign skills, political writing, the budget process, and other such practical subjects. The institute also offers workshops, classes, and seminars for nondegree candidates. And, as you might expect, there's also an intern component to the program.

Similar opportunities for study are offered by the Center for the American Woman and Politics of the Eagleton Institute of Politics at Rutgers University in New Brunswick, New Jersey. The center is basically a research and information-collecting

Jill Ruckelshaus, of the National Center for Voluntary Action, speaks at a conference on women in presidential campaigns.

Connecticut State Senator Audrey Beck (seated) and former Delaware State Senator Louise Conner speak with students at Rutgers University's Visiting Program in Practical Politics.

center but also offers workshops in such subjects as budget processes and federal programs, which provide practical training for women in politics. The center has brought in female politicians to teach courses and live with the students. The program has proved so successful that the center is encouraging other colleges to adopt similar programs.

The Eagleton Institute itself offers a graduate program in applied politics. Every year the institute awards 15 to 20 fellowships to candidates for the master's degree in political science or another social science at Rutgers. The program includes participation in an internship, an independent-study project, and seminars.

Betsy Crone, a 30-year-old Washington-based campaign consultant, attended Eagleton after a year of unsuccessful job hunting, even though she had a bachelor's degree in political science as well as campaign experience. Today she believes, "If I hadn't gone to graduate school, I might have spent the rest of my life as a typist."

I wanted a combination of academic credentials and practical application and Eagleton offered it. If you're interested in practical politics, it's one of the best places to go. I worked as an intern for the Twentieth Century Fund on a project involving campaign-finance reform. There were useful courses on the legislative process and political parties, which emphasized their practical aspects. A lot of current politicians participated in the program. Eagleton is small, so everybody knows everyone else, and they have connections around the country. The dean knew Matt Reese, a Washington political consultant, which led me to a job with him. I had learned about voter analysis and about computers at Eagleton. That helped me get the job with Matt Reese.

If you want to specialize in campaign politics, there are courses in such techniques as polling, media, and election targeting. Jill Buckley, a Washington media consultant, combined volunteer campaign experience with a background in advertising and marketing. Courses in marketing, advertising, and survey research are useful tools in a job such as hers. A combination of film production courses and campaign experience is also good background for media work. If you want to work with the press, public relations and journalism courses are valuable.

Pollster Dottie Lynch, now senior analyst with Cambridge Survey Research, majored in sociology but chose political topics for her research projects. Her master's degree is also in sociology with emphasis on public opinion analysis. She interned in NBC's elections unit while a graduate student and then was hired full time. She advises academic work combined with campaign experience as the best route for an aspiring pollster.

Women in office often say they wish they had learned more about economics, accounting, and computers. They suggest going heavy on courses in business, budgeting, and computer science in undergraduate school.

Academic credentials are important. And, today, that means *graduate* credentials. A bachelor's degree is taken for granted. Graduate programs in public affairs, public administration, political science, economics, business, or a science won't guarantee you a job but it will help. It might be wise to establish yourself as an expert in a technical field rather than join the thousands with master's degrees in political science. Still, most politicians are generalists and rely on experts for any technical information needed. Anyone in politics has to be able to learn a new subject quickly and to move from one issue to another easily. The ability to write simply and clearly is an important skill for most political professionals. Nancy Lewinsohn, chief of staff to Governor Ella Grasso, says the academic training she received in getting a Ph.D. in history was useful because it taught her to analyze data and discipline herself to think and work hard.

There are prestigious academic programs that are worth investigating. A degree from the Kennedy Institute of Public Affairs at Harvard or the Woodrow Wilson School at Princeton is an easy ticket to high government jobs.

White House and congressional fellowships provide the opportunity to work inside Congress and the White House. They receive a stipend, not to mention an impressive credential to add to their résumé. Between 14 and 19 White House Fellows are selected every year, but competition is tough. In 1976, for instance, only 17 were selected out of 2,864 applicants. (Interestingly, a law suit charging the program with sex discrimination was pending that year, which may account for the fact that 8 of those 17 were women.) But state legislatures and organizations also offer fellowships. Another directory published by the National Center for Public Service Internship Programs lists internships, and fellowships for the graduate, postgraduate, and midcareer professional (see Appendix).

If you are interested in a professional political career, academic credentials do more than help get you a job. They go a long way toward establishing you as a professional. Jill Schuker, executive director of the New England Congressional Caucus, combined academic credentials with political expertise. She has a master's degree in political science and received a Ford Foundation grant after graduate school to work in the Massachusetts legislature for the minority leader.

"I never worked as a volunteer or secretary. I think graduate school and the grant established me as a professional. There were few women in those programs so I stood out. I built on each position, and one thing led to another. (Of course, if you can't deliver, you are found out very quickly.)"

Probably the best education for a political career is a law degree. That doesn't mean that legal training is necessarily the best preparation, but many men in politics are lawyers and they tend to favor people who speak their language. Because so much of a politician's work involves the law, particularly if you work for a legislative body, a law education surely can't hurt.

For women, a law degree is instant proof of competence and training. Joan Claybrook, chief lobbyist for Ralph Nader's Congress Watch before President Carter appointed her to head the National Highway Traffic Safety Administration, says the law degree is an advantage, particularly in working with legislation. Joan's credentials included a congressional fellowship and four years with the National Highway Traffic Safety Administration, but she still felt she needed a law degree.

"To be creative and imaginative with public policy, I had to understand the design of it. As a woman I needed better credentials to continue to attain the positions I wanted. As a lobbyist, it's a big advantage. I can make decisions myself without consulting a lawyer. That makes me more effective."

A career in law can be advantageous to a politician because it permits a flexible schedule. Many lawyers, when they are elected to office, take a leave of absence from the law firms that employ them. They may still earn a retainer from the firm because their reputation aids the firm in getting clients. They also have time off for legislative or city council sessions.

Washington is a lawyer's town: one resident in 34 is a lawyer, whereas, in California, the state with the highest proportion of lawyers, only one resident in 831 is a lawyer. More than half the members of Congress are lawyers. Of 19 women members in 1976, 9 were lawyers.

Congresswoman Pat Schroeder believes that her law degree has forced some of the other members to take her seriously. "The minute a woman runs for office everyone wants to know why she is qualified. With fewer qualifications than your male opponents, many of whom are lawyers, you're less credible. You don't need a law degree to be effective, but it makes some members take you seriously."

Generally, those officeholders and professionals with law degrees believe it's a great asset, but those without it say it makes no difference.

Maryland State Senator Rosalie Abrams is a nurse with a master's degree in political science. She entered politics because she was appalled with the conditions in Maryland hospitals. She's had a tremendous impact on health care in Maryland.

Doris Bunte, assistant majority leader of the Massachusetts House of Representatives, having been elected by Boston's black Roxbury community, says she got her degree from "the school of hard knocks in a course called survival." Bunte was a high school drop-out who finally received her diploma in 1968, when her own children were in high school. Earlier in her career, Bunte organized a citywide public housing tenants' association in Boston and was director of the city's housing authority. She's now in demand to teach college courses. In the 1975–76 academic year, she taught in the Harvard Graduate School of Design as a Loeb Fellow.

Whether as an officeholder, lobbyist, or legislative assistant, to be successful in politics you need to understand the issues facing your constituency, the politics of getting elected, and how government works. Most older women in office today got their basic training through political party work or from the League of Women Voters. Working for a party teaches the practical aspects of politics; the league trains you how to research and analyze issues and to lobby for them.

"My preparation for Congress came from many years of involvement in my community," says Martha Keys. "I organized an open-housing campaign and worked for other community goals. I learned how the political machinery works by working within my party. I ran campaigns, which is the best preparation for a candidate. I never planned a career in Congress, but I saw that if I really wanted to change things, I needed to be in on the decision making. I am not a novice about government. I don't feel disadvantaged."

Mayors Janet Gray Hayes and Lila Cockrell were both members of the League of Women Voters who decided the league didn't go far enough. County Councilwoman Ann Stockett, a former league president in Anne Arundel County, Maryland, also served on the county's Charter Revision Commission. "That experience gave me an advantage I couldn't put a dollar value on. I feel far better prepared than some people there. I think there's a great advantage in starting out in local government and moving on."

Connecticut Secretary of State Gloria Schaffer says the traditional wife-mother role is relevant today as preparation for a political career. "Our dollars are being spent on sewers and roads, health care and education. Married women with children often have the best training and background for what you need to know once you're elected."

Other kinds of community involvement may lead to a political career. Congresswoman Barbara Mikulski, who before her present job served two terms on the Baltimore City Council, was a community organizer with a degree in social work. Elaine Noble, a college teacher in Boston before her election to the Massachusetts legislature, had become disturbed by the unresponsiveness of city government to her community's needs. "A few years ago, I didn't know the difference between City Hall and the Statehouse. I learned as a matter of survival for my community. By starting with a little exercise like saving a playground, you learn a lot about politics." Elaine turned her campaign headquarters into a community center where she's teaching other women how to organize politically.

Cathy Bertini was an accomplished organizer by the time she was 25. Cathy began organizing at 15. Ten years later she was youth director for the Republican National Committee. In 1976, Cathy was hired to manage a congressional campaign.

At 15, Cathy attended a "TAR"—Teenage Republican School. After a one-week course, she went home and organized the first Teenage Republican Club there. By the time she reached college, she wanted a full-time political career. She chose Albany State University because of its nearness to the state capital.

I was a political science major but nothing I learned in books can compare with what I learned in practice. Any high school student can organize a Teenage Republican Club. In college, I organized a Students for Rockefeller group and got 3,000 students to attend one rally. I worked in the state legislature and in Governor Rockefeller's office and received course credit for it. After graduation, I was offered the job of youth director of the New York State Republican Committee. Getting involved in a political party is the best route to a political career.

Most successful political women have at one time worked in political campaigns, usually volunteering to work for a candidate they believe in. Whether you want a career as a campaign consultant, a legislative assistant, or a congressmember, there's no better crash course than a campaign. It's also a way to meet people who may help you build a political career. If the candidate wins, you may be offered a staff position. A campaign is to politics what basic training is to military life. But it's a lot more fun.

"You get into a campaign because you believe in the candidate," says Barbara Shailor, field director for the Energy Action Committee. While working as a stewardess, Barbara volunteered in several statewide campaigns in Colorado and was hired as "advancewoman" in Fred Harris's low budget 1976 presidential effort. "A presidential campaign can give you a four-year degree in six months. If you're persistent, your participation will evolve into other things."

4
Working for an Officeholder

Short of getting elected to office yourself, in politics, the closest place to the action is as close as you can get to the officeholder.

There are a wide variety of jobs to be done on the staff of an elected official. But do not expect job security in any of them. All staff positions are exempt from civil service protection, so how long your job lasts depends on the whims of your boss and the electorate.

Most staff positions require long hours and hard work. If you work for a public official who is driven by a desire to achieve, you will be expected to have similar drive. If your employer is public minded, aggressive, and capable of delegating authority, your job will be a constant challenge. It is important to work for someone you admire and whose views and goals reflect your own.

"He demands that you squeeze out every bit of energy you have," said Betty Rainwater about Jimmy Carter. Ms. Rainwater's salary jumped from $12,000 to $42,500 when she moved from deputy press secretary in his campaign to a White House staff job. It is a never-ending learning process to be around him."

Working for an officeholder is an awesome responsibility. A wrong move can mean losing the next election. Most public officials rely heavily on their staffs for political advice and support as well as for substantive work such as research and policy making. Most officeholders are only as competent as the people around them.

"A rule of thumb is if something goes wrong, the staff gets the blame," says a former congressional aide. "When something goes well, the congressman gets the credit."

You can put your boss in the history books, but few people will know about your contribution. You will always play a behind-the-scenes role. Some aides tire of never being their own person, never running for office themselves. Others enjoy being influential in government policy making, without having the burdens of running for and holding office.

And just how much of that influence you're able to wield depends on your access to the elected official. Since most public officials are men, it is no surprise that their top aides are also men. Even women in professional jobs sometimes find they have a more difficult time getting to their boss than their male counterparts. Often the job may demand traveling with the officeholder, and a woman is not asked along. Whom you work for is terribly important. And if it is a man, you have to be concerned about his views and personality—and his ability to work with a professional woman. Some men are simply unable to delegate substantial authority to a woman. One clue to what his views on women really are is what roles other women play on his staff.

The functions of a staff reflect the function of the officeholder. If the latter is an executive—a governor, mayor, or county executive—most staff members will play administrative roles. They will help shape and administer policy. This usually involves overseeing the hundreds or thousands of employees who make the government work. These workers are called bureaucrats, and the government agencies are the bureaucracy.

A legislator's staff is primarily involved in doing research and writing legislation. That means developing a good idea into a workable law. A legislative assistant also works hard to get the law passed. Legislators spend a lot of time solving their constituents' problems. An aide, or "caseworker," will act as a liaison between the citizen and the government agencies.

Margaret "Midge" Costanza, assistant to President Carter, serves as the President's emissary to organized groups.

If you work as an aide to a state legislator or city council member, you will earn a low salary and may not work at all except when the body is in session. When Barbara Mikulski was a member of the Baltimore City Council, she was given an allowance of $2,000 to hire an aide. To that sum, Barbara added $5,000 from her own pocket. An alderman (the term used for a city council member) in Chicago gets $12,000 for an assistant. Alderman Martin Oberman pays one assistant $13,500 and another $9,000 from money he raises at events. An aide to the Anne Arundel County delegation to the Maryland General Assembly earns $13,500 and receives no benefits. During the session, the legislators receive less than $150 a week to pay an assistant.

Most executives have special assistants to handle everything from press to legislation, as well as cabinet members who run the government departments.

President Carter has appointed more women to high-level jobs than any other president. Carter's is the first cabinet to include two women: Juanita M. Kreps, an economist, is secretary of commerce, and Patricia Roberts Harris, an attorney, is secretary of housing and urban development. Only three women previously served in presidential cabinets. More significantly, Carter placed and encouraged his deputies to place, a substantial number of women in policy-making jobs in the departments and agencies of the federal government. He named Lucy Wilson Benson, former president of the League of Women Voters, the first woman under-secretary of state in that department's history. Of all political jobs, those at the White House are most prestigious. Carter's record regarding the White House staff is better at the mid-level than at the top. Three women are on his "senior" staff: Midge Costanza, assistant to the president for liason; Martha "Bunny" Mitchell and Esther Peterson are presidential special assistants.

Margita White, the first woman director of the White House Office of Communications (under President Gerald Ford) found working for the President unlike any other political job. "I was always aware I was working for the president. You expect perfectionism from yourself and your colleagues. He deserves the best."

The chief of staff in an executive office is the most powerful person next to the executive. In a big city like Baltimore, that person has 43,000 employees to worry about and nearly one million people to serve. Joan Bereska met Baltimore Mayor William Donald Schaefer when she was an advocate for a housing organization and he was on the city council. "We were civic pixies together," recalls Joan. When Schaefer ran for council president Joan was his campaign manager. When he won the election, she became his executive assistant. Now she is administrative officer for the city—the only woman in the country who is chief of staff to a big-city mayor.

> Essentially, I do whatever the mayor does and whatever he tells me to do. Because this mayor works fourteen to sixteen hours a day and isn't married he sometimes forgets other people have other places to go. I sit in on cabinet meetings and help him make policy decisions. I hire staff. I keep an eye on the bureaucracy, making sure everything moves in the right direction. I am the person who passes the orders to the staff members. I tell them they work for the mayor, but they do what I tell them, because that is what the mayor wants. It takes all the energy the mayor has to keep this city moving.

Joan earns $29,000 a year and doubts she will ever have a job with more authority. She is committed to the mayor's programs.

"I am in on the grand plan. That means making Baltimore a city that is proud of itself. It is enormously challenging. A big city is a big business today. What is exciting is to run a city well and bring new, wonderful things here. The mayor and I share a commitment to turn the city around."

Nancy Lewinsohn is chief of staff to Connecticut Governor Ella Grasso. Nancy was Grasso's administrative assistant in Congress and took a $2,000 pay cut—from $31,000 to $29,000—when she moved from Washington to Hartford. During the first six months of the Grasso administration, Nancy worked 12 to 14

Connecticut Governor Ella Grasso speaks with Nancy Lewinsohn, her chief of staff.

hours a day and on weekends. Now she works about 10 hours a day and several hours on Saturday. She is the boss of the governor's purposefully small six-person staff. She undoubtedly has more power now than before.

> As chief executive of a state, you have the responsibility of making sure the state agencies serve the people. I carry the governor's message to the agencies. I see that they carry out her goals. I absorb what is going on and tell her about it. I make it possible for her to use her time to the optimum. Every staff member tries to lighten her burden. I know her well enough to know what she should hear and what she does not have to hear. My job is to give her the support she needs.

Geri Pleshaw has served in administrative and policy-making jobs on the staff of Boston Mayor Kevin White. For two years, Geri was the mayor's special assistant on women. It took two years for Geri and women's groups to hammer out an affirmative-action plan to spur the city agencies to hire more women. Then Geri had to sell the plan. "I had to pressure the right people. Policy making does not end with a good program. It takes a lot of political work to see it through. Not everyone agreed that we needed an affirmative-action policy. I had to convince them it was the mayor's policy."

Geri's present job is administrative. She coordinates the mayor's activities with other mayors, Washington, and the Democratic party. Geri's pace is hectic. She crams a beauty shop appointment into her lunch hour. Her telephone rings constantly, and the door to her office opens every five minutes.

"I do everything that no one else does," she explains. "I make sure the right things get done and the right answers are found. I am often here late at night."

Working in a big-city administration, where politics has never been a genteel sport, requires a thick skin and good survival instincts. "If you mess up, you get screamed at," says Geri. "You have to prove you are competent. The mayor gives you a lot of freedom and you must use it wisely. I was timid at first, but now I argue with him. Still, I defer to him. The people who get killed here are the ones with overbearing personal ambition. They want to be close to him all of the time."

It is not fun to be the only woman on top. Even though Joan Bereska has a law degree and two master's degrees, there are men who cannot accept her authority. For years, Joan had to put up with political gossip that made her the mayor's girlfriend.

> When I was moving up, a woman could not have her own personality. I had to act like a man. I could not let my feminine side show—that was taken as a sign of weakness. It is a constant struggle. A woman has to prove herself again and again. The names do not bother me anymore. I am tougher than I used to be. What bothers me is going home tough. This job takes its toll.

Launching a professional career on a congressmember's staff can be equally demoralizing. Capitol Hill has been a notably sexist environment. A survey of Senate offices by the Capitol Hill Women's Caucus in 1975 showed that 30 offices lacked women in professional jobs. Overall, men earned 75 percent of all professional salaries, and women in professional jobs earned an average of $6,000 less than men. Congress passed a law barring sex discrimination in federal agencies and then exempted themselves from the law. Efforts at reform have been unsuccessful.

A problem to be faced by anyone seeking a job on the Hill is that every office is a private king or queendom. Most congressional offices have a receptionist, a personal secretary, a secretary who answers bulk mail, several legislative assistants, an administrative assistant, and a press secretary. Senate offices generally have many more persons doing similar jobs. Salaries are arbitrary. A legislative assistant may earn $21,000 in one office, and her friend down the hall may do the same job for $12,000.

Getting a professional position is extremely difficult. Competition is stiff. The Hill is filled with energetic young people who are ambitious and highly competitive. For a woman, the experience of moving into a professional job can be particularly embittering.

After graduating from college Amy Levy came to Washington because she wanted to change the world. "My options were to drop out or to change things."

Amy worked as an intern for six months earning a low salary but having a lot of responsibility. She worked on legislation and constituent mail. She had access to the congressmember, who, as it happened, shared her idealism and gave her opportunities to do meaningful tasks. But when she went out looking for a real job, she found that the only positions available were typing jobs. In four years, Amy moved from one office to another. She was a typist earning $6,500, a legislative secretary, and a secretary in the press division, earning from $7,800 to $9,000. She was fired from one job and quit the other jobs. It's not hard to understand why along the way she became a feminist.

In one office, women had to answer the phones. The congressman got angry if a man answered the phone. Women were expected to come in on Saturday and answer the mail, but the men didn't have to. In another office, women were expected to wash dishes. If the congressman stayed late, there was a "late girl" on duty. Even professional women served as "late girls." When an administrative assistant asked me to get his breakfast, I quit.

Amy stuck it out. She was persistent and kept her ears open for better jobs. She did more work than was required; she worked longer hours than necessary. "I was ambitious. I wanted a career. I took the knocks and kept plugging. I wanted the power to influence a member, and you do that if you are a professional. But you have to decide that reaching your goal is worth it."

Amy was eventually hired as press secretary to Congressman Joe Moakley of Massachusetts. Moakley was looking for a feminist. His political views are liberal and meshed with Amy's. Amy did legislative work on women's issues as well as press relations. She recently left Washington for a reporting job on a small newspaper in Maine.

"He and I agreed on issues, so anytime I felt like being creative and wanted to do legislative work, I could. From that point of view, I was where I wanted to be. I reached my goal. People treated me differently, but it was anticlimactic. You have to be such a fighter that you get burned out. You also learned that you cannot have that much impact. You are one person among so many."

Of course, many women are happy and feel well paid in traditional "female" jobs, and derive a special satisfaction simply to be involved on any level with the workings of government. Joyce Foristel found her job as a personal secretary to a congresswoman far more satisfying than working in a mail-order house. "I thought working in Congress was the most fantastic thing in the world." She earned $14,000 a year and resigned when she became pregnant.

Joan Burda, however, was another who could not put up with a job as a $5,600 "robo typist." She was a college graduate and running an automatic typewriter machine was boring. Her next job was also clerical but included some legislative research. She stuck that out for a year and a half, until she moved to another office as a "caseworker." Being a caseworker is also a "female" job, but Joan enjoyed it.

"I like helping people. The job is like social work. I work with the federal agencies such as the labor department and social security in solving people's problems. About 85 percent of all caseworkers are women. The job is a valuable learning experience, but it is not something you would want to do forever." After a year in the job, Joan quit to go to law school.

Shelley Fidler learned the political and legislative ropes running the Boston chapter of the Americans for Democratic Action. When she came to Washington, she knew she wanted a job as legislative assistant. Shelley refused many typing tests. It took her six months to get a job as a legislative assistant, earning $21,000, to Congressman Phil Sharpe, a 33-year-old freshman and former political science professor. She oversees five other workers on Sharpe's staff. They are two legislative aides, who earn about $12,000 and primarily do research; an editor, who writes a newsletter to constituents; a secretary, who answers mail in volume on the robo-typewriter; and an intern, who performs clerical jobs and works on legislative projects.

Shelley finds her job challenging and rewarding. Sharpe is a genuinely nice person and demonstrates his confidence in Shelley's abilities. A good legislative assistant is creative, flexible, and politically wise. Many congressmembers, it is said, are only as good as their best legislative assistant.

A day on the Hill with Shelley is varied and non-stop. "My job is never boring. Here are the events of a typical day. Met with other members and their L.A.s to discuss energy priorities; met with lobbying groups to get support for the clean air act; wrote a letter about a special constituent inquiry; asked for research material from Congressional Research Office; wrote several press releases and my energy newsletter; attended a committee hearing and took notes; and, as always, met with Phil several times during the day."

It took Shelley about four months of research, digging, and brainstorming with Congressman Sharpe, before she wrote an amendment to an energy bill. The amendment requires auto manufacturers to increase the fuel economy of their cars and establishes deadlines. After writing the amendment, Shelley put her political skills to work to get the legislation passed.

The idea is to influence four hundred and thirty-four other people to agree with Phil. Some of the L.A.s here, particularly the lawyers, feel insulted about getting into the political side of the operation, but I think that is a shortcoming. What you do is organize. You find everybody who agrees with you, and they find other people, and you coordinate your efforts until you have a lot of people spreading the message. You are trying to get information out so people will begin to believe as you believe. We lobby other members. It is like a campaign. The most important thing is to be right, and then to make it happen. What is most rewarding is the knowledge that I am helping to serve the needs of people.

When Congress is in session, Capitol Hill buzzes with excitement. There are always throngs of people around. You feel as if history is being made every minute.

It is that way nearly 24 hours a day in the office of Congressman Robert Drinan of Massachusetts. An activist priest and leader of the peace movement, Father Drinan has a national constituency. His administrative assistant, Ranny Shuman, seems to make sense out of the chaos that dominates the office atmosphere.

Ranny was an anti-war activist in college. After graduating and returning to her home district she worked in Drinan's campaign. She planned to stay with the campaign until she found a job, but her volunteer position turned into a staff job when the assistant campaign manager became ill. That was five years ago; Ranny never left.

Ranny works for a man she respects, who gives her total freedom in running the office. She uses her organizational skills to reflect her point of view, and the office she has organized is more egalitarian than most. The staff members do their own typing, and everyone, even the receptionist, handles some legislative work. No one—not even lawyers—are excluded from lunchtime shifts at the receptionist's desk. Ranny keeps the office moving, and advises the congressman on political decisions.

"You can never walk away from the job. I am on call all the time. It gets frustrating because you move so quickly from one thing to another. But I like the pace. I am never bored. I am here because Drinan is brilliant and I agree with his views. I am doing something valuable by working for him."

There are other difficulties a woman in politics has to face. For instance, just because she is hired for a professional job doesn't ensure her the authority to match the title. She may have to fight a constant battle to get responsible tasks. There are many women who left the Hill because they never won the battle. Another problem is having less access to the congress-member. Power emanates from the boss, and without access to him or her, your role is limited, particularly in the Senate. Staff members in the Senate have more power because the senators rely on their assistants more, but the staffs are larger and more competitive. Because the Senate is an all-male club, women tend to get lost.

Moreover, for anyone to get ahead, a certain aggressiveness is required. And while it is taken for granted that a man will promote himself to gain a higher salary, more responsibility, or a better job, when a woman is ambitious, she may be called pushy, and denied her rightful advancement. So women have to learn the extra skill of how to be aggressive without being "threatening."

Elinor Bachrach wanted a higher salary and a more prestigious position. She was an L.A. to Senator William Proxmire, and had previously worked for another House and Senate member as an L.A. It was time for her to move up. That meant getting a position on a committee staff. Committee jobs usually command higher salaries. You work for 25 members instead of only one, and you have more independence and more say in the legislation that gets passed. "I made it clear I wanted it," says Elinor who now works for the Senate Banking Committee, which Proxmire chairs:

> You have to go after everything you want. I wanted an interesting, influential job, and I wanted the professional credential. It is not enough to be a woman in a professional job. You have to push on, and make it clear you will leave if you are not treated right.
>
> Working on a committee gives me the chance to become an expert. The job is much more substantive. I handle my own legislation and run hearings, and people interested in an issue come directly to me. It is fun to be an L.A., but most people do not stay in that job for more than three years. You want to move up. A job on a committee is potentially more long lasting.

When she came to the Hill looking for a job, Elinor had all the course credits toward a doctorate in political science with only the dissertation remaining to be done. She was hired by the congressman from her home state of Maine, who was later elected to the Senate. That was a lucky break for her, but she had to use her lucky break to good advantage to move ahead. "Moving to the Senate gave me a much broader horizon. Senator Hathaway was on the Banking Committee, which put me in touch with the Proxmire staff. You get to a certain position and then you cash in your chips. You tell everyone you know that you want a better job. But as hard as it is for anyone, for women it is always harder."

Other specialized jobs on Capitol Hill offer greater power and independence and more visibility than a job on a member's staff, and a few women have risen to these positions. Pat Goldman is executive director of the House Wednesday Group, a study group of liberal Republican members. Jill Schuker is executive director of the New England Congressional Caucus. She earns about $24,000. Pat works for 33 members, Jill, for 25, including the Speaker of the House. Since power is having access to powerful people, it follows that working for 25 members instead of one gives you more power.

Jill was hired as the first person to direct the New England Caucus. The job has given her executive skills and enhanced her political sophistication.

The first year I had to overcome some confidence gaps. Working for 25 members, all but one of whom were male, meant there would be some suspicions about my abilities. I worked hard to overcome that. I made sure I was on the right track and that they were happy with the way things were going. That took balancing and juggling, especially since I work with members of both parties. In this job, I combine skills of legislative assistant, press secretary, and administrator. I do press and fund raising, write memos and speeches, prepare questions for testimony, and put together issue papers. The job has been a challenge for me. It has given me good background in administration. I believe I have created a useful institution. But this is not the end of the line for me. It's another step up.

5

Political Parties

The ideal national committeewoman must be a handsome lady, able to introduce the president gracefully, and wear orchids well. She must never interfere with party policy.

Edward J. Flynn
Democratic National Chairman [under
Franklin D. Roosevelt]

The National Women's Political Caucus was organized . . . when women in the movement realized that equality for women would never come about unless women held positions of power within the party structure.

Jane McMichael
NWPC Executive Director

Our two national parties have been bastions of male dominance. Both Democratic and Republican parties have been exclusively male clubs. Membership for women was restricted to the "federations" and "auxiliaries," armies of dutiful foot soldiers to send out into battle at the next election but never to be consulted.

"How can we sit in the same room with a woman?" asked a New York City Democratic leader in 1967, urging his colleague to defeat female party worker Ronnie Eldridge's claim to a party office. "We've never had a woman inside the ward office before," explained a Chicago Democratic committeeman when asked why I had been told to leave the headquarters and denied

40

information on vote totals on election night, although I was there as a newspaper reporter.

Even as recently as 1975, the proportion of state party leaders was overwhelmingly male. In that year, only five Democratic and three Republican chairpersons were women. "It's a system of institutionalized male domination," says Ken Bode, political writer for the *New Republic* magazine who served as research director of the commission that reformed Democratic party rules and opened the door to minorities and women. "The state party would make a rule that the chairman conduct the party's business and the vice-chairman oversee the women's auxiliaries and social events. Obviously, the rule was designed to maintain the status quo."

After women won the vote, both parties elected to have a committeeman and a committeewoman from each state. These national committee members now constitute the parties' governing bodies. Traditionally, however, the women were placed on the committees by men and were never expected to act independently.

Since the formation of the National Women's Political Caucus, women have organized within both parties to give women a voice. Koryne Horbal, chairperson of the Democratic National Committee's women's caucus and a committeewoman from Minnesota, has found her job difficult. "The biggest percentage of women in positions of power made it there through men and don't have their own agenda. They don't want to open up the process to other women because it's a threat to their own position."

Given that fact, Koryne has performed miracles. You could see her influence, and that of other feminists at the 1976 Democratic convention. Though there were fewer women delegates there than in 1972, they had more clout. A woman served as convention chairperson for the first time. A pro-abortion plank was included in the platform. Women were promised a strong voice in a Democratic administration. Most important, the feminist wing was given control of the women's division, a holdover from the days of women's auxiliaries.

Mary Louise Smith rose through the ranks of the Iowa Re-

Mary Louise Smith, chairperson of the Republican National
Committee, at a conference.

New chairperson of the Democratic National Committee
Lindy Boggs addresses the Party's 1976 Convention.

publican party. She served as the first woman chairperson of the National party from 1974 until after the 1976 election. No one believed she would survive a year. Her presence has benefited women within the party ranks and in staff positions at the national committee.

"If someone had told me that I would be party chairman I don't know if I would have known what they were talking about," this 60-year-old grandmother told the *Washington Post*. "You see, there is no way anyone can ever tell a woman or anyone who is black, 'If you do this and so, you'll be this.'" Though white herself, Mrs. Smith understands the lack of faith both groups have in their chances for advancement.

Smith says her politics are moderately conservative. She helped organize the Iowa chapter of the National Women's Political Caucus. "There's nothing revolutionary about being a feminist. It's the natural thing."

If you want to have political influence, you should become involved with your local party. The two parties determine to a large degree who our public officials are. They find and groom candidates, and then organize to get them elected. Even an "independent" usually seeks party endorsement in the general election. With that endorsement come financial contributions and the troops who ring doorbells.

Every four years the party nominates its presidential candidate at a national convention. Delegates are elected who may be committed to one candidate or another. The party writes a list of priorities called a platform and party rules. Every group tries to advance its own goals. They solicit the nominee's promise to support their goals after he is elected and to appoint their choices to high government positions. Only recently have women played a role in the process of selecting a candidate or had their interests included in the platform and endorsed by the nominee.

You can achieve power in the party in one of two ways. You can work as a party volunteer and win election to party office. Or you can work as a professional on the staff of the state or national party. In either case, you will discover it's more difficult if you are a woman.

Women in professional jobs as well as those who volunteer their services are working to bring more women into the political process. While they work within their parties, they also work together for a common goal that extends across partisan lines. Many of these women are members of the National Women's Political Caucus, which helps bolster their strength within their respective political parties.

Both Koryne Horbal and Mary Louise Smith were "party regulars." They climbed the party ranks by volunteering to ring doorbells for candidates. Gradually they rose from positions in county leadership to the state office to positions on the national committee. Horbal proved herself as a worker. When she became state chairperson, she organized a statewide campaign that brought the party into a position of prominence. They elected a Democratic governor and gained a majority in the legislature. Suddenly Koryne became controversial. She expressed her feminist views, and organized a feminist caucus that took over the party.

"I finally had the self-confidence to speak for women within the party. I could have climbed the ladder and pulled it up after me. But after what I went through as a woman working her way up from the precinct level, I couldn't close my eyes. I had to make it easier for the women who would follow me."

Women who work on a party's staff discover a similar atmosphere. Professional women at the Republican National Committee organized for better salaries and responsibilities. "The minuses outweigh the pluses for a woman. Many men don't know how to handle an aggressive woman," says Cathy Bertini. "You have to do your job well. I never do anything that would give someone cause to say, 'there is a typical woman.'"

Not only is it difficult to land a job in the party ranks, but there's no security in working for the party either. Party chairpeople come and go, and like presidents, each brings in a new regime. New positions may be created and then crumble. Mary Louise Smith created five positions to bring new groups into the party. Cathy Bertini was hired as youth director and told her job would last at least two years. But after a year, when funds were needed for campaigns, her job was eliminated.

Working for a national party is the next best thing to being involved in a nonstop political campaign. Competition between the two parties never lets up. The nation's eye is focused on the national committees. In a presidential election year, staff is added and the headquarters becomes an adjunct to the campaign.

Monica Borkowski has survived many regimes since she arrived at the Democratic National Committee in 1969. At that time, the party was recovering from an unsuccessful presidential campaign. The entire party was $8 million in debt. Monica, who had worked on Capitol Hill for eight years, felt like a pioneer.

"The party was in such bad shape, I thought the most productive thing I could do would be to come and work here. It was like joining the Peace Corps. There really wasn't a functioning headquarters. Hill offices seemed luxurious by comparison. There were months when we didn't know if we would get paid. I worked for the executive director, Bob Keefe, who was a political genius. It was exciting to watch him put the party back together. I felt a part of it."

Monica moved from one secretarial or administrative assistant's job to another. In 1975, she was given a professional job as co-director of the Compliance Review Commission, and a salary of $13,000 a year. She works with state parties to bring traditionally underrepresented groups into the party. It's a time-consuming, emotionally draining job. She works long hours and weekends. But she prefers the political atmosphere at the committee to working on the Hill. She believes she is fulfilling her goal of public service.

"I never felt I was in a political environment there. Here there is always something new to be done. You're always selling the party and articulating the party's position. Even when there is no election, you are preparing for the next one. I think my work has more of an impact here. It's important to encourage people to believe in the party process and to participate."

Staff positions with both parties are basically the same. Both have a chairperson with a staff of assistants, an executive director, and people assigned to help the groups who make up the party's membership, such as state chairperson, women, minorities, governors, and mayors. There's also a research department, a campaign office, a communications department to handle press relations, and a finance office.

If you choose to work for a party, you must put the party before any issue or candidate. Party people believe in the party's ideology and in the two-party system. They may support one candidate in a presidential primary, but when a different candidate is nominated, the party person works for that candidate's election. And salaries are notoriously low.

Chris Hurtz, a staff assistant to Mary Louise Smith, has that sense of party dedication. She handled press for the Iowa party. When Mrs. Smith came to Washington, she brought Chris with her. Chris travels with Mrs. Smith, handling press relations on the road. She does "advance" work—making arrangements before Mrs. Smith arrives—and "political backgrounding"—giving Mrs. Smith information about the district, and the party in the district, they are visiting. Last year, Mrs. Smith conducted training seminars around the country. Chris spent all but three weekends away from home.

> Working for a local party office gave me the experience to empathize with people in the community. But working in Washington is more exciting. I work evenings and weekends. You have to believe in the party and want to contribute to the party's future. You can't change the numbers of Republican voters overnight. I tell my friends to choose a party and get involved. You can begin at the local level and have a marked effect on the leadership of your community.

Not all party positions are pure politics. Jane Hartley directs the Democratic Mayor's Conference. She is well informed on the issues that concern the country's mayors. She combines that background with organizational skills she learned in political campaigns, skills she learned from the nation's best politicians —the mayors. Milwaukee Mayor Henry B. Meier was impressed with her work as a lobbyist for the U.S. Conference of Mayors.

Soon afterward, she was hired to organize the Mayor's Conference and become its director.

> I had to start from zero and develop an organization. The strategy was to bring the mayors into the national committee and give them a political organization to work through. One of our priorities was to develop a national urban-policy statement. The mayors would use the statement in addressing presidential candidates. When the candidates asked the mayors for manpower, money, and support, the mayors would have something to request in return. I organized regional conferences in a number of cities. Our other primary task was to put together a network of mayors to involve them in party activities, in order to have more power at the convention. I also opened up communications with the Congress, to give legislators an idea of the needs of cities and to give the mayors better access to Congress.

Jane works 10 hours a day, sometimes longer. She earns $16,000 a year. Although she doesn't deal specifically with women's issues, she believes that her being a woman helps the women's cause. "I'm making the mayors more aware of women's capabilities and their special problems."

What you do for a state party depends on the size of the staff, which in turn is contingent on the power of the party in the state. In New York State, the party chairman wields enormous power. Esther Newberg turned down higher-paying jobs to remain the party's executive director because of the power it gave her. Eventually, a new governor took over the party and Esther was out of a job. "It's important for women within the party to see other women in meaningful jobs. Because I worked for a strong chairman, my suggestions to include more women carried substantial weight."

In Maryland, the Democratic party organization plays a minor role. The chairman is a mouthpiece for Governor Marvin Mandel who is the party leader. The party office has one person on staff, and that person, Janet Engle, is bored, frustrated, and turned off to politics. She works about 25 hours a week and earns $7,500.

"There is nothing exciting to do here. I see things we could do, and whenever I suggest them, they say 'when we have more money.' I stay because whenever I become totally discouraged, something happens to raise my hopes."

Under such circumstances, it isn't surprising that Janet, who is finishing her undergraduate work this year, has decided against a political career. "I've decided I don't have the personality for it," she says. "I like things to be structured, with definite rules and procedures. In politics, you have to play a lot of games. When you work for a party, you can't take sides. You must take the party's point of view. You do things because someone owes you something or you want something from somebody. Often who you know is more important than what you know. You have to devote so much time to it. It requires an undying love and I don't have that."

Cathy Bertini preferred working for the state party in New York to her job at the Republican National Committee. She had more power. She enjoyed working with young people and turning them on to politics. At national headquarters, the young people she dealt with were already leaders. She acted as a consultant on a one-time basis rather than over a long period of time.

"I preferred organizing at the grass roots because the effects of my work were more obvious. It's satisfying to work for a candidate, but when you train young people you are leaving a legacy. You're building new leadership into the party. At one Teenage Republican Club, we invited two boys who wanted to mess things up. After a week, they got turned on and went back to serious work. It's nice to have the power to change things."

6

Lobbying and Related Jobs

There are other ways of influencing the decision-making process without holding office, being on an officeholder's staff, or working for a party. It isn't in a vacuum that the president, Congress, and the executive agencies make laws or set policies. They listen to the nation's many interest groups before they make decisions.

Washington is the organization capital of the world. Business and labor leaders, farmers, doctors, teachers, consumers, minority groups, women, and an endless stream of other pressure groups keep a watchful eye on Capitol Hill. They want any decisions that affect them to reflect their interests. The special interests representing big corporate dollars have for a long time had overwhelming influence over Congress.

Politicians are equally concerned about how pressure groups react to laws and policies. They understand that these groups reelect or defeat them. They also understand that implementing a law or a policy is easier if the affected group contributed its views. Even governments—those of the counties, cities, and states—and other government agencies want their voice heard on Capitol Hill.

For this reason, pressure groups have offices in Washington and hire representatives to speak for them. These representatives are known as lobbyists.

"If lobbyists didn't exist, they would have to be invented," says Jane O'Grady, the one-person Washington lobby for the Amalgamated Clothing Workers union. "Lobbying is a two-way street. We 'lobby' members of Congress on issues we consider important. But they also lobby us. They know the labor movement is powerful and that I am in close communication with other labor lobbyists. We channel information back and forth."

Lobbyists are an essential part of the legislative process, but their public image is poor. They have been seen as "buying" public officials with expensive dinners, campaign contributions, and even payroll checks. The special interests representing big corporate dollars have for a long time had an overwhelming influence over Congress. To help curb lobbyists' abuses, more stringent lobbying-disclosure laws were passed and public financing of campaigns was introduced.

Despite this unsavory image, most lobbyists work hard, are knowledgeable in their field and respected by congressmembers and their staffs. Lobbyists are an invaluable source of information, and often do research that members don't have the resources for.

Traditionally, there have been few women among professional lobbyists. The League of Women Voters and other civic organizations have sent their volunteer members to Washington and state capitals to lobby for government reform, education legislation, and tax relief. But corporations have few women executives, trade unions have few women officers, and the professions tend to place men in top administrative jobs. As a result, their lobbyists have also been male. Women have only recently been considered capable of dealing with—or appropriate to—an almost totally male political world.

Jane O'Grady recalls that few women were making the trek between Senate and House lobbies when she arrived in Washington in 1964. She and Evie Dubrow, lobbyist for the International Ladies' Garment Workers' Union, represent unions whose members make clothing and, as you'd expect, are mostly women. So it's not surprising that those unions were the first to hire women lobbyists.

Barbara Fauser, of the Civil Service Employee's Association, presents a memorandum outlining CSEA's position on several bills to State Assemblyman G. James Fremming. New York State's largest public employees union, the CSEA places strong emphasis on political lobbying to attain legislative goals for public workers. At right is Ramona Gallagher, another CSEA lobbyist.

Mattie Jackson, Vice-President of the International Ladies' Garment Workers' Union discusses a problem regarding imports with California Representative Phillip Burton.

Mary Gereau, an old-timer, who earlier lobbied for the National Education Association and is now lobbyist for the Treasury Employees Union, says she was a freak in those early days. "It helped to be different, but I wouldn't have lasted a minute if it hadn't been that I knew what I was doing. I think women tend to be more persevering and therefore make excellent lobbyists. But you don't last long if you think it's a flirty situation," says Gereau, who won't wear pants on the Hill, even today. "I'd say about one percent of the lobbyists now are women."

Penny Farthing, one of a new generation of women lobbyists, is an attorney with the Federal Trade Commission. Penny lobbied for the American Retail Federation before joining the FTC. She says there are problems for women lobbyists, but none that can't be overcome. "They say they'd rather talk to a woman, which can make things a little lighter, but can also work to your detriment. They can say, 'Here comes that bubble-headed girl.' It's hard to be charming and hard working at the same time. You want to be convincing without being overbearing, because we're in the minority up there. The principal staff on nearly every committee is all male. But if you produce workmanlike products, they respect you."

There are several reasons to consider a job as a lobbyist. First of all, lobbyists are generally well paid. If you're interested in a high salary, you could become a lobbyist for a corporation or trade association and make a substantial salary right from the start. Many lobbyists are lawyers who represent several corporate clients and earn $100,000 and more a year. A lobbyist for the American Medical Association earns around $50,000 a year. Union lobbyists with considerable experience, such as Jane O'Grady and Mary Gereau, earn around $30,000. Beth Landau, a lobbyist for the American Federation of State, County and Municipal Employees, earned $18,000 when she first arrived in Washington. Rae Fork Evans, a lobbyist with CBS, earns $20,000. Men who lobby for corporations generally are vice-presidents in charge of government relations, and earn much more. Penny Farthing earns about $28,000 a year with the

Federal Trade Commission. Even lobbyists for Common Cause, a public-interest organization, earn from $18,000 to $32,000.

Common Cause, however, is an exception. Most public-interest lobbyists are underpaid. Carol Burris, director of the Women's Lobby, receives a salary that barely covers her expenses. When Joan Claybrook, head of the National Highway Traffic Safety Administration was director of Congress Watch, Ralph Nader's lobbying arm, she could have been earning $50,000 as a corporate lobbyist. Her job with the federal government, which she gave up when she went to work for Nader, would have been paying her about $30,000 today. She earned about one third of that with Congress Watch. "I was paid enough but I had no luxuries," she says. "You have to be devoted and want to do it. To represent the public interest, you have to make a choice about your life-style."

The public-interest lobby grew up in the late 1960s as a means of voicing the concerns of individual citizens. The groups pay low salaries because they rely for their existence on contributions from their members. These lobbyists believe in the cause they are working for. If they didn't, they wouldn't be there. Joan Claybrook worked 12 hours a day and took work home.

"I have always believed it appropriate for citizens to get their point of view across and try to influence public policy. I come from a family where it was natural to fight for citizens' rights. I view what I do as an obligation. I think I am lucky. Anyone who can mesh personal concerns, ambitions, and viewpoints with his or her role in the public sphere is lucky. Ralph calls it 'full-time citizenship.' "

It takes a lot of determination to be a lobbyist. If you believe in what you are lobbying for, it is a lot easier.

"Lobbying can get to be a day-to-day drag, unless you have a commitment to the issues," says Jane O'Grady. "If you can't do the trek between the House and Senate two or three times a day, you aren't going to get very far. I believe I would be worn out if I weren't fortified by an intensity about an issue. I couldn't work for just anybody. I have to work within the sphere of social concern that corresponds with my values. I don't think of this as a job. It's part of my life-style. My concern is for social change. What I am doing is important."

It's difficult to imagine working on Capitol Hill without a liking for the frenetic pace. If you are there because you believe in what you are trying to accomplish, the excitement is its own reward. And a lobbyist can feel as much a part of that excitement as a member of Congress or a staff person.

Jane O'Grady's enthusiasm about her work is infectious:

When there is a specific bill coming up for a vote, I will concentrate all my energies on it. For instance, last week the House was voting to override the president's veto of an emergency-employment bill. You can imagine how important that was to the labor movement. We worked together in a coalition. We did a head count of all the members and divided them up. I did nothing but knock on doors for three days, speaking to members and staff. On the day of the vote, I walked the lobbies, speaking to whoever came off the floor.

It is exciting when a bill is voted upon that you care about. It may be a close vote, and you want to see what will happen. In the 1960s, when the civil rights legislation was developed, it was exciting to be here. I was part of a whole new era in our history.

Working as a lobbyist is gratifying because you can have a direct effect on legislation. A lobbyist, like a legislator, has to be creative and politically astute. Some lobbyists have worked their way into the position through the organization they represent. Others are hired because they have worked on the Hill as a legislative assistant or on a committee staff. They have developed political expertise and know how the Hill operates.

Mary Allen Jolley obtained her knowledge about vocational education working for a congressman who headed an education subcommittee. She also learned the politics of legislation. No wonder the American Vocational Association hired her to lobby for them. Mary negotiated every word of the Vocational Education Act of 1968. She now earns $30,000 a year as director of public affairs for the American Home Economics Association.

"You learn that you have no votes on the committee. You

have to talk the bill through and develop it with the staff. You must let them know it's their bill. You have to anticipate all the controversies in advance and negotiate them. When it is finished, the bill has to be something that nearly everybody can favor. You have to know when to give in and when not to give in."

Even without a passionate commitment to a cause, a lobbyist's job can be rewarding. For Rae Fork Evans, who previously handled press relations of CBS News' Washington Bureau before stepping into the corporation's government relations office, the move to lobbyist has been an education in the legislative process, the broadcast industry, and communications law. "There is always something new to absorb. The amount of reading I have to do is phenomenal. I'm lucky. My boss is patient and lets me make my own mistakes. I used to drag stuff home and have my lawyer-husband help me analyze it. But now I can do it myself. I've learned how the Congress works and what it takes to be effective. I am never bored."

There are also lobbyists who represent governments and government agencies. Because Penny Farthing works for a government regulating agency, she can't lobby in the normal sense. She can't buttonhole members and ask them to vote a certain way. But she can comment on legislation as congressional liaison for the Federal Trade Commission. The FTC protects consumers from the deceptive practices and monopolies of corporations. Penny is an attorney who finds lobbying a challenging career. Though most lobbyists are not lawyers, Penny feels her legal training is invaluable.

"Law is the best training for a lobbyist because it is the nuts and bolts of a lobbyist's activities. You work with the law intimately. If I weren't a lawyer, I would constantly be seeking a lawyer's opinion. What I like best about my job is having the chance to change the law. I directly affect the quality of citizens' lives that way."

Another government lobbyist, Susan Tannenbaum, Washington representative for Connecticut, is one of a handful of women who run a state office in Washington. Susan was hired because of her political experience which includes having worked for Senator Robert Kennedy, former Congressman Allard Lowenstein, former Ohio Governor John Gilligan, as well as on then-Senator Walter Mondale's presidential campaign staff. Susan started out in Washington with a bachelor's degree and used every job to improve her political skills.

Susan advises Connecticut congressmembers of the state's needs. She is a liason between state and federal governments. She has learned to be more pragmatic working for a state government than she was when she worked on the Hill for crusaders like Kennedy and Lowenstein. When Mondale received the vice-presidential nomination, Susan took a leave of absence to work as deputy press secretary in his campaign. She is a political professional who enjoys running her own office, but she sometimes misses the frenetic pace of the Hill and campaigns.

> Some of the great crusades are over. Lowenstein did so much for congressional reform; Kennedy was so compassionate. Today, you must understand what can't be done. Working with a state government, you become less idealistic, more pragmatic and patient. In every job I have held, I took on more responsibility and learned more skills than I had in the previous job. In this job, I have to initiate whatever is going to happen. I like having that authority. It's nice to know you don't have to lean on anybody. I like this job because I can start a project and see it finished. I am an information specialist and a messenger. I serve the state and the governor. I'm not as idealistic as I used to be, but I wouldn't lobby for General Motors.

If you work for an organization, you may have the responsibility of educating your members out in the field in political matters. "Having a million members to ring doorbells on election day is far more valuable than money," says Mary Gereau. "Without a politically mobilized membership, a lobbyist's job is far more difficult."

That's why the labor lobby is so powerful. Congress knows that labor can command millions of votes on election day. Some unions have people who do nothing but organize the members for political action. Others, such as the Amalgamated Clothing

Workers Union, use their lobbyist for that purpose. Jane O'Grady spends about half her working hours informing the unions' members about pending legislation and mobilizing them to "lobby" their congressmembers. She wants the congressmembers besieged with phone calls and letters at the same time Jane is lobbying them on Capitol Hill. She often travels long distances to speak to her unions' members.

Some organizations have people who spend all their time traveling around the country organizing the members politically. While Mary Gereau was lobbying on Capitol Hill for the National Education Association, Jean Parlett was traveling to school districts getting teachers involved in politics. Jean began in 1966 when there was only one person in the national headquarters performing that task. The year before, a poll of teachers had revealed that they thought it undignified for teachers to be politically active. Jean worked for seven years convincing them to become a political force. In 1972, she directed NEA's successful political campaign for a Congress sympathetic to education.

"We targeted 42 districts, and selected Democratic and Republican candidates to support. In some districts, there were 50 different teachers' organizations. We had to put these groups together into a functioning organization. We hired political consultants to train the teachers in campaign techniques. When the votes were in, it was obvious we had made a big difference. For example, Senator Claiborne Pell of Rhode Island said that he would not have won without us."

Jean's starting salary was $11,000. When she left NEA in 1973, she had two full-time assistants and ten people working part-time in regional offices. Her salary was $26,800. Her title was director of political education. "It was great to be part of something from the beginning and then watch it grow. I felt I was making the country a better place. I have six children and my husband is a teachers' advocate. I cared about what was happening in the classroom and knew it was a political issue. To be good at my job, I had to care and believe that the political process is terribly important."

For women like Jean Parlett, Jane O'Grady, and Mary Gereau,

lobbying involved a commitment to the organization and the issues that the organization espoused. Jane O'Grady can't separate her job from her personal life. "Working in the milieu of the trade-union family is a total way of life," she says. But for Beth Landau, whose background was politics, lobbying for the American Federation of State, County and Municipal Employees union is a poor substitute for a full-time political career. She spends half her time lobbying on the Hill and the other half organizing members for political activity.

"Politics is in my blood and I can't get rid of it. I would prefer a job that was more directly political such as running a campaign. I don't feel I have a future here. A union hierarchy is like a bureaucracy. I don't see any place I can move."

Political organizations hire people for other tasks besides lobbying and organization building. If the organization is small and has a limited budget, the director will get a minimal salary and do everything from writing press releases to lobbying and fund raising. She will keep contact with the membership and do the bidding of the organization's board of directors.

Jeanne Cronin was a Democrat and social worker before she decided to come to Washington and begin a political career. Today she is managing director of The Ripon Society, an organization of progressive Republicans. She wants the organization to play a more aggressive role in politics.

When I began, I was told what my administrative duties were. I report to the national executive committee. My administrative work involves promotion, providing information to our members, keeping the books, and being a spokesperson for the organization.

When I first came there, the organization was limited in scope. I came up with ten projects, and the executive board has responded positively. Ripon is a voluntary organization with chapters around the country. I want the national office to be a catalyst for the chapters' activities. To coordinate their activities, I wrote up a report sheet for each chapter to use to keep us informed. I want us to support candidates and lobby for legislation.

Shelley Fidler, legislative assistant to Congressman Philip Sharpe, began her political career in Boston when she answered an ad in the paper that read, "Politics with Pay." The job was executive secretary for the Boston chapter of the Americans for Democratic Action, a liberal organization, and her starting salary was $6,000. By the time she left, her title was executive director—the same as the man who had preceded her—and her salary was closer to $10,000.

"Working for ADA was the most important job I ever had. It got me interested in the legislative process," says Shelley, who majored in art in college. "It also introduced me to knowledgeable people. It gave me the exciting opportunity to develop and exercise political skills. ADA is a respected organization, and I was automatically respected as their representative. I did everything from run the mimeograph machine to write speeches and legislation. Everything I know, I learned in that job."

Working for a large political organization means that jobs are specialized. Common Cause, the "citizen's lobby" has an organization chart that looks like a corporation's. Salaries range from $8,500 to $38,000. A large grass-roots membership of 280,000 supports the organization with annual dues of $15. That adds up to about $4 million a year.

Ruth Saxe is one of the vice-presidents. When she first arrived, the organization was only six months old. She had no idea what her job would be. A divorcée with two children, Ruth had a lot of rotten jobs before she was hired at the Peace Corps. She spent seven years there, ending as chief of the Caribbean program, responsible for more than 500 volunteers in 11 countries. She was hired at Common Cause to set up a program directing volunteers.

"I began with nothing but the names of 1,200 people who wanted to help. I had to convince the staff that we could give them real jobs. We now have 300 people working here every week, and at interesting jobs such as research or monitoring legislation."

Ruth created Common Cause's "Washington Connection," a

communications network of people in every congressional district who are the backbone of the organization. When a bill comes up in Congress, the Washington Connection contacts a person in each congressional district who activates Common Cause members to mobilize public opinion around the issue. Now Ruth is involved in management decisions for the entire organization. She is in charge of membership development and communications and earns $28,000.

"My job is fascinating because there are no prototypes. Everything I do I make up as I go along. I am managing our direct-mail campaign and our membership-building program. I develop new techniques as I do things. It's an enormously high-energy job."

A small cluster of women's organizations that grew out of the feminist movement is bringing women from the sidelines of politics into the fray. The Women's Lobby in the persons of Carol Burris and Maya Miller is speaking out on women's issues on Capitol Hill. They have become a voice for poor women who never had a spokesperson before. The Women's Campaign Fund is run by Carol Randles. In 1976, she directed a fund-raising effort that proved that women will support women candidates with money as well as words. The National Women's Political Caucus is organizing women in both parties to increase women's participation in the government process. The Caucus has organized chapters around the country. One arm of the NWPC, the National Women's Education Fund, is educating women to move onto the campaign trail. Its executive director, Betsey Wright, built the organization from scratch and is working to develop a women's political network around the country. She hopes that by ten years from now, there will be no further need for the Education Fund.

Betsey grew up in southwestern Texas. Her father was a physician who cared for poor Mexican-American families when other doctors refused to. Betsey's political inspiration came from those roots. She is driven by a passion to bring outsiders into the process. She organized voter registration drives in Texas and worked for Frances "Sissy" Farenthold, a candidate for governor and a people's advocate in the Texas legislature.

Betsey became involved in the women's movement in reaction to the treatment of women in male-dominated Texas politics.

If I could find another way to change society, I would reject politics. It is a chipping away process and you do not make changes very fast. I do not like politics but I am motivated to political action because it is the only way I can find to make progress. I do not know of another way to make change happen. Most male politicians have let me down. That is why I am interested in developing more women politicians. My lifetime career pattern has been to bring more people into the political process. It has been a passion with me. I have always been concerned that so few people participate. Now I am motivating women to carry their leadership potential into the public sphere. I hope that in ten years, we won't be needed. But my tasks seem endless now.

7

Working for Campaigns

A political campaign is hectic and intense. It is like working in a pressure cooker: the process lasts only a short time, but the results are extreme—and final. There is no time for regular meals or sleep, or for all the things that need to be done. Strangers are expected to work as a unit in a highly charged atmosphere. Decisions are made that leave no room for second thoughts.

Some people are drawn to campaigns just because of that intensity. They are addicts, who drift from one campaign to another. Some people emerge every four years to work for a presidential candidate hoping they will at last pick a winner and get a taste of power. But most people burn themselves out after a few campaigns and, by choice, change to a more stable existence.

But if you want a career in politics, there are many good reasons to join a political campaign, the most important ones— aside from electing your candidate—having to do with the skills you will learn and the people you will meet. Working in campaigns is the union card of politics. You meet people with similar views. You learn the workings of politics. You prove yourself. And from that foundation, you can build a career that makes you a highly valued commodity.

Every major campaign has a staff that includes a manager

and a deputy, a press secretary, a scheduler, a research or issues director, a field coordinator, field organizers, a director of volunteers, an advance person, a treasurer, and a fund raiser. The number of campaign offices and staff depends on the geographic area the campaign must cover and the nature of the campaign. A city council race covers a small area and some people may even perform more than one function. A presidential campaign has a large national office and an office in every state and congressional district.

"Everything I know, I learned as a volunteer," says Anne Wexler, whose political career began as a volunteer in Democratic politics in Connecticut. Anne helped forge the reform wing of the party in that state and then moved into national party affairs. In recent years, she transferred her political experience into the job of associate publisher of *Rolling Stone* magazine while continuing to play an active role in the presidential campaign of Jimmy Carter. After Carter's election, Anne moved to the transition team staff and is now deputy under-secretary of regional affairs for the Department of Commerce.

"A campaign takes in every aspect of unit management," says Anne who built a reputation as a campaign manager in Connecticut politics. "You learn finance, organization, writing, and leadership. You must know how to motivate people. You can never overlook any detail. At *Rolling Stone,* I organized college promotions and radio spots. A good campaign person is often perceived as good at campaigning and nothing else. I think a campaign is the best training for any kind of career."

Jackie Smelkinson worked in numerous campaigns before landing her present high-level staff job. She established herself as a hard worker and an exceptional organizer, who knew the ins and outs of Maryland politics. She was always in demand.

In a campaign, you begin by mobilizing a few people. One person can energize ten; ten, a hundred. It involves recognizing people's abilities and challenging them to produce. I was a precinct worker and made phone calls in my first campaign. Of two hundred people, if I could convince one hundred, that was

Maggi Peyton, Deputy Campaign Manager in Bella Abzug's 1977 race to become New York City's Democratic mayoral candidate, works with volunteer assistants Zoe Myers (left) and Debra Fried (right).

a tremendous reward. I did my job in an orderly fashion and kept records.

The next time, I helped a candidate for the U.S. Senate. I was a precinct captain and got other people to make phone calls. The campaign after that was for governor. I was headquarters manager, responsible for the entire operation.

In 1974, when Jackie's friend Ted Venetoulis decided to run for Baltimore county executive, everyone said he didn't have a chance. Even though at the time a woman campaign manager was practically unheard of, Jackie did the impossible.

"This was an experiment and a challenge. We had very stiff competition. We waged a low-budget campaign and used people as multipliers. We didn't want to spend money on TV and radio. If you need contributions from fat cats, you have to make deals. We weren't willing to do that. We started in my living room with twenty-three people. By the end of the campaign, we had six thousand. Ted went everywhere to meet people personally. We won the primary by a landslide, and no one was more surprised than we were. In the general election, we ran against a state senator who was groomed for this position. He spent $200,000 and we spent $50,000. When we won, it was a thrill for us all."

Even now, as Venetoulis's chief of staff, Jackie continues to use her campaign skills. She delegates authority. She is his political adviser and helps him develop strategy. "Whether planning a campaign or making a policy decision, in developing strategy, you have to think of all the possibilities. Whenever you are surprised, you know your strategy has been poor. Ted makes the decisions, but I help him think them through."

Jackie had become a respected campaign manager despite having worked in many losing campaigns. It was not until she worked for Venetoulis that she managed a winning campaign. And the prize was a staff position.

Women have more difficulty getting hired to work on staff after a campaign ends than their male colleagues. For instance, it was not until Jackie Smelkinson was asked to run a presidential campaign organization in Maryland that she asked for a salary.

"I reached a turning point in my life," says Jackie, who was typical of older women who had spent years doing volunteer work in campaigns. "I decided that one of the limitations of being a volunteer was the view others have of you. I decided that to do a professional job and serve the candidate best, I should be paid. I knew he would view me with more respect and he would not have to worry about hurting my feelings or keeping me satisfied. I had no problem getting the salary. And it was a big ego boost for me."

While men are generally "taken care of" after a losing campaign, women are forgotten. Betsey Wright who worked in many campaigns in Texas found that her male friends somehow always had jobs between campaigns, while she was left jobless. That is because women are generally not viewed as professionals, or included in the male political network.

But it is foolhardy for anyone to join a campaign expecting a job to come from it. The aftermath of a losing campaign can be very depressing. No matter how good a candidate's odds seem to be, there is no sure way of predicting a winner to work for.

"When I worked for Dick Ottinger's 1970 campaign for the Senate and he lost, I felt a personal defeat," recalls Beth Landau.

I was assistant to the campaign manager and I worked day and night. If he had won, I would have had an important position on his staff. I knew his defeat was not my fault, but you always think you might have done something else to make him win. The most trying part for me after a losing campaign is being out of work. Nobody knows you after a losing campaign. I was unemployed for a year. That convinced me I wanted a more permanent job.

Tresa Smith was recuperating from a Senate campaign when she got a phone call asking her to join the presidential campaign of Senator Henry Jackson. She had been semi-retired for six months, living at her parents' ranch, and was ready to come back to Washington. She knew it meant working seven days a week and giving up her personal life.

"I was hired as director of field coordination, a campaign job I had never done before. It was a challenge to make things happen the way we wanted. I was the contact point for all the state coordinators. You learn so much with every campaign. I was really ready to get into it."

The first time I phoned Tresa, she was too busy to return my call. By the second time, a few weeks later, Jackson had pulled out of the race. The job had lasted about a year.

"There was no guarantee how long the campaign would last," said Tresa, back home after a morning spent on the unemployment line. "I was surprised and disappointed when the senator quit. But I do not think I wasted my time. I learned a lot. Right now, I am tired and want to go into hibernation. It is a crazy way to spend your life but I have never done anything else. I do not know what I want to do next."

Tresa was hired as an organizer because the Jackson campaign wanted to place a woman in a high, policy-making position. Her salary was $20,000 a year. Not long after the Jackson campaign folded, she was hired on vice-presidential candidate Walter Mondale's staff. In 1976, for the first time, presidential candidates recruited women for professional tasks. Apparently they had felt pressured to have women in responsible jobs, if not to consult them on strategy.

More women were also hired as managers of congressional campaigns that year than ever before. Rather than accept positions in traditionally female roles—fund raiser, coordinator of volunteers, or scheduler, for instance—women were demanding managerial jobs with salaries and titles commensurate with their responsibilities. Women have often managed campaigns before, but because they were volunteers and not included in the candidate's inner circle of advisers, they were viewed as "office managers" rather than campaign managers.

Ann Lewis was recruited for Senator Birch Bayh's presidential campaign as deputy campaign manager at a salary of about $30,000 a year. Although she was not negative about the experience as deputy—second in command—it convinced her that she would have to be first in command in her next job. And, in fact, she was hired to run a congressman's office.

Ann believes the best way to begin is to find a local candidate, even if at first it means volunteering. Most campaign workers start at the bottom. "A local campaign is the best way to start because you can learn so much more. You'll have the opportunity to learn everything. If you do it well and you meet people, they will come looking for you." If you begin when you are in high school or college, you can demand a salary by the time you have graduated and need one.

Ann had always wanted to work in politics but thought the only way to pursue her dream would be to marry a man who was equally interested. "When I was growing up, a woman had to express herself indirectly—through a man." The experience she had gained as a politician's wife helped when her marriage broke up. Starting out as an all-around office assistant for Boston Mayor Kevin White, she worked her way up to the position of White's special assistant before joining the Bayh campaign.

You never know where a campaign job will lead. "My present job is the result of what I did for Fred," says Barbara Shailor, who after working in several local campaigns in Colorado, left her job as a stewardess to become advance woman in Fred Harris's 1976 presidential campaign. "I gave up $12,000 to work for Fred because I believed in him and because I knew if I were persistent it would establish me as a political professional."

A presidential campaign is the most grueling and stressful of all campaigns. The stakes are the highest. Nothing tests your endurance more—or your capabilities. Nothing is potentially so destructive—or so rewarding. Presidential politics are notorious for power plays and for once-in-a-lifetime experiences.

Barbara was hired as field director of the Energy Action Committee the day after Harris's campaign folded. "I think it is best to start in a local campaign. A presidential campaign is a sink-or-swim situation. It could be a frightening experience for someone who has never worked in politics before."

And of all the difficult jobs in campaigning, advance work is one of the *most* difficult. Barbara traveled to 55 cities seeking coalitions of supporters for Harris. She was constantly on the road. As a matter of fact, she is now organizing those same citizens to lobby against the powerful oil industry. Besides organizing Harris supporters, Barbara had to arrange every detail of her candidate's visit a few days ahead of him. She had to worry about press coverage, getting a podium, and "turning out a crowd."

"It was the most phenomenal experience of my life. You feel a sense of urgency all the time. You have so little time to accomplish all that has to be done. A presidential campaign never goes home."

I can laugh about it now but the most harrowing experience I ever had was when I arrived in Sacramento two days late. We had planned a rally on the steps of the state capital. We expected fifteen hundred people. I met our local contacts and discovered they had spent the money we had allocated for invitations on a balloon with Fred's name on it. I had to scramble for thirty-six hours to put together a crowd. Fred was supposed to speak at noon. At eleven forty-five all the national and local media arrived, and I had no idea how many people would show up. There was a blue-grass band blaring music on the capital steps. The supreme court was in session, and the justices sent the police to quiet the band. We found out that the hot-air balloon was illegal. The buses we had rented to get people there went to day-care centers and brought in a hundred and twenty-five four-year-olds, with the cameras rolling. Believe it or not, though, a thousand people showed up and it was a huge success.

"Issues adviser" Jessica Tuchman, a Ph.D. in molecular biology, had to school presidential contender Congressman Morris Udall on a whole range of issues, from a national welfare program to whether the navy should go for a carrier-based fleet or a submarine-based fleet. One year before the first presidential primary, Jessica had threatened to quit. She was working 70 hours a week.

"It is the hardest job I can imagine—and the most rewarding. When I want to know something, I pick the best people in the field and spend an hour with them. Then I write memos and position papers. If you are interested in substance, this is the most mind-expanding job in the world," said Jessica, now head of the National Security Council's Global Issues Office.

The presidency is the prize that makes superstars out of unknowns. When, in 1972, Jimmy Carter decided to enter the race for the presidency, he was an obscure governor from Georgia. But he knew he would be out of a job in two years and have plenty of time to campaign.

The deputy press secretary in the Carter campaign, Betty Rainwater, now a White House deputy assistant, taught dance and was a secretary before she became intrigued with Carter and joined his 1970 gubernatorial campaign as a receptionist. When he won, Betty went to work in the governor's press office and soon moved into a more responsible press job. What began as a lark became a political career.

"When I got involved in his first campaign, I wanted to observe him but I never thought he would win. It became more serious and meaningful the longer I worked with him. He demands so much of you. Watching him has been a never-ending learning process in itself."

Betty got on-the-job training in Governor Carter's press office. She and press secretary Jody Powell set up a national press operation for his Presidential campaign. They traveled with the candidate, made sure the press buses kept their schedule, and kept the journalists reasonably happy. The deputy press operation for his presidential campaign. They traveled cluding every word the candidate is saying so she can explain it to other people. For a woman, there are special frustrations.

"You have to constantly remind people, when they get a little sexist and forget you, not to leave you out of meetings. Usually, though, it is not intentional and is straightened out with a few words like 'you forgot to let me know . . .' The real problem is people from the outside who cannot believe a woman holds a position of authority," says Betty who now works for Hamilton Jordan, President Carter's special assistant.

You may enjoy putting together a campaign or become adept at a particular aspect of campaign organization. But you may tire of the total immersion of campaign work. One alternative is to become a campaign consultant. You will still work long hours during the campaign season, as well as experience the tension and excitement. However, you will be paid more than the campaign staff and can escape the day-to-day details and the internal power struggles.

Political consultants spend their time helping people win elections. Most have small consulting firms or free-lance. They provide expertise based on experience. People can be found to knock on doors and stuff envelopes, but for more sophisticated things like polling and putting the candidate on television, they need an expert.

"A consultant has a special kind of authority," says Betsy Crone. "I tailor the plans of a campaign to its needs. Because I lack the vested interest that the campaign staff has, I can see situations more objectively. They are paying me for that. I have no enemies and no ax to grind."

Campaign consulting is a growing field, though few women make a living at it. One difficulty is finding work when campaign season is over. Between campaign jobs, most campaign consultants work for organizations, businesses, or officeholders. During the campaign season, they spend more time on planes than on the ground.

Betsy, who worked for an established consulting firm for several years, now free-lances and prefers it. She likes being her own boss, working for whomever she pleases, and putting in as many hours as she wants. Betsy earns from $100 to $150 a day, so if she doesn't work every workday she can still pay the rent. She has a part-time steady assignment doing fund raising for the National Women's Political Caucus, but she maintains a stream of individual political clients, too.

"It is best to first learn everything and then specialize," explains Betsy. "I became a fund raiser when the firm I worked for was handling a campaign in Hawaii and I wanted to go there. They needed a fund raiser, so I became one. Everybody needs fund raising, and no one does it very well. I like it because I know whether or not I've been successful.

"I also specialize in voter identification and targeting. I have developed my own system of learning which voters you need to persuade. You lose some of the excitement when you work as a consultant, but there's a lot of satisfaction to be had from doing the job well."

Jill Buckley, a partner with Joe Rothstein, is a highly paid campaign consultant. Jill met Joe when she was a campaign volunteer and he was a consultant for Colorado Senator Floyd Haskell, and came to work with him when she moved to Washington. She had been working in marketing and advertising and volunteering in campaigns, and had never thought about a career that combined politics with her professional experience.

Jill and Joe have won some long-shot races. They never have to seek out clients—candidates come to them. When the campaign period ends, Jill and Joe help new congressmembers set up their offices.

They specialize in media and strategy. It's an unusual combination but their round-the-clock schedule during campaign season proves that it works.

How you use paid media is important. You must decide what your message is. What should people know about your campaign and your candidate and your opponent? What are you trying to do? Whom are you trying to reach? The undecided voters are the people you want to address. Then you decide how to communicate that message. We might decide, for instance, on six 30-second television spots. We may use scripts or simply follow the candidate around, directing him through the scene we want to convey. Then, we hire someone to edit it. We charge from three hundred to five hundred dollars a day. We advise on strategy and how to best allocate their resources. We save people money that way.

Public-opinion polling is another technique that helps a campaign allocate resources. More is needed than merely a knowledge of survey research. You must understand politics and the workings of campaigns as well. Survey research can help a campaign decide whether to invest scarce funds in media or field organization. You learn which issues are important to the voters and whether they think the candidate can solve those problems. You learn where the opponent is most vulnerable. You need campaign experience to understand how a poll is used, and which information is useful.

Dottie Lynch, now a senior analyst with Cambridge Survey Research, a polling firm, understands those issues. She took her present job because she wanted to continue to participate directly in politics.

While working for NBC News' elections unit during the 1972 presidential campaign, Dottie met Pat Caddell, a 21-year-old Harvard student who was polling for candidate Senator George McGovern.

"My friends were involved in protests against the war and I felt guilty for not participating. I decided I was more interested in helping elect McGovern than working for NBC." The night McGovern won the nomination, Dottie quit her job and went to work for Pat.

Betsy, Jill, and Dottie are selective about whom they work for. Generally they work for candidates they want to see elected. Although Cambridge Survey Research, the organization polling for Jimmy Carter in 1976, works for corporate clients in off-election years, Dottie will handle only political clients:

I am interested in electing better candidates and improving the quality of politics. I don't want to help corporations make more money. Everyone here is young, and works hard, and is dedicated. Our field director oversees the interviews and we have people do data processing. I do the analysis and the questionnaires and work directly with the campaign. When a survey comes in, I work on the analysis until ten or eleven in the evening. Then I report to the campaign and help them make strategy decisions. It is a complex task to take ten thousand pages of computer printout and in a week or ten days produce an analysis that makes political sense. How much extra time I give the campaign depends on how much I believe in the candidate.

Not all campaign consultants or consulting firms work independently. Both national parties have campaign services divisions that consult to Senate and House candidates. Political organizations often provide consultants to campaigns.

Anne Canby, director of the campaign services project of the National Committee for an Effective Congress, sends out consultants to progressive candidates in both parties. Anne is like a doctor. She decides which consultant to send where, and then follows up after the consultant leaves.

"I have to cope with crises constantly. I am in touch with the campaigns of all the various candidates and available on a twenty-four-hour basis. Dealing with the crises of twenty-five campaigns can be hairy."

Anne was press secretary to Congressman Paul McCloskey before being hired to organize the campaign services project. She has been offered other jobs that would pay more than the $18,000 she earns, but stays because she likes the pace and the sense of accomplishment. "It is more action oriented than working on the Hill. I believe we must attract the best candidates to run for office. Often the best people do not have the funds or expertise to get elected. I am making my contribution to society by helping elect good candidates." Anne also uses her influence to aid women candidates.

Wilma Goldstein directed survey research for the Republican National Committee before taking her present job as deputy campaign manager for the Republican Congressional Campaign Committee. Wilma does not believe that campaign consultants should cross party lines. She believes in the two-party system and says she is strengthening it by concentrating on electing Republicans, even though some candidates don't support women's issues. Wilma has a permanent virus: "Politics. I love it." She prefers working for hundreds of candidates to working for only one.

"I work seven days a week under grueling conditions. But it is different from working on one campaign. You get to a point where you want to work on a different level. Here I decide on the best overall strategy for a whole range of campaigns. The decisions are broader, and I don't have to do the same thing over and over again. I am more useful here making objective decisions about a number of campaigns."

8

Running for Office

"Anyone who announces for public office has taken a step onto the auction block," says Betsey Wright, who trains women to run for office. "For a woman, it is especially difficult. The first time a woman presents herself to the public, it is terrifying."

Placing yourself on the auction block takes courage for anyone, but getting elected to public office is even more difficult for a woman. It is taken for granted that a man is a serious candidate. A woman has to prove it. It is assumed that a man can win. A woman is thought of as a loser. If a woman needs party support, she must fight twice as hard to get it.

That doesn't mean that women *are* losers. In recent years, women have scored smashing victories. The electorate has begun to see women candidates as more honest and less power hungry than men.

What are women waiting for? Why is 54 percent of the electorate content to hold only 5 percent of all public offices? Why were there no women in the U.S. Senate and only 18 women in the 465-member House of Representatives in 1977, one less woman than in 1976? Why are there only two women governors? With all the women PTA members, why were only 13 percent of the school-board seats filled by women in 1976? Only 9.1 percent of state legislators are women.

"It takes guts and stamina to run," says San Jose Mayor Janet

Gray Hayes, who defeated six men to become the first woman executive of a major city. "What my victory did was give women the final edge of encouragement."

Hayes served on the city council for three and a half years and was vice-mayor when the mayor's seat became vacant. "I didn't see anyone who could do a better job. I came from the ranks of the citizens and I understood the problems and frustrations they felt. That background gave me an understanding of the issues and one of the necessary qualifications to run for mayor."

When Pat Schroeder, a young lawyer with two small children, decided to run for Congress in 1972, many people said that she should start with a local office and work her way up. "They don't tell a young man to do that," says Congresswoman Schroeder. "My answer was you start at the top. You dispel the myth that a woman with young children cannot be in Congress. You prove it can be done.

"In 1972, there were no women on the Denver city council, none on the school board, and only one in the state legislature. Now there are two on the council, three on the school board, and eighteen in the one-hundred-member legislature. We even have a woman secretary of state. That is an incredible gain in two years. This year, we have women running for everything, including county commissioner."

The greatest obstacle for women is lack of confidence. Men are taught to see themselves as leaders. Women lack that sense. Running for office necessitates overcoming feminine conditioning.

"Having made the decision to run, I went home a little shaky," says Massachusetts Representative Doris Bunte, who defeated two incumbents to represent the black community of Roxbury in Boston. "I looked in the mirror and said 'who do you think you are? What makes you think you can do a better job than someone else?' I made the decision that I was at least as capable as some people I had seen. I knew if people were supporting me then I had to tell it like it is. I had to relay the needs of my community."

Nor does society make it any easier for women to overcome

their lack of confidence. To some people, both men and women, running for office implies a rejection of the wife and mother roles, and they give women candidates a hard time.

"My husband called a news conference and ran my campaign from his law office," says Oregon Representative Nancie Fadaley, the wife of a state senator. Nancie ran for the legislature in 1970 when the one woman representative from the county resigned.

> At first, I thought, "I am running for his political future. I am not going to do anything to hurt him." Everyone said, "Ed Fadaley is running his wife." And I too thought he was making the decisions. But then I realized I was the one who was walking through the streets, meeting the people, writing the press releases, making the speeches. I had been his legislative assistant for ten years, writing his press releases. I hadn't realized I could run for office myself.
>
> Over and over again I was asked about my children. Anytime I made a speech, I worked it in that my mother lived with us, so my kids would get a meal if I was late. People said, "I would like to vote for you but I worry about your children."
>
> I had to prove I was the one who was running and that I was capable of the job. But I didn't have that feeling then. After I won and served for a while, I gained the self-confidence. Now, I know that I can do it.

Since Nancie Fadaley's first race, the climate has changed. In 1972, no one asked about her children. In 1974, she and other women candidates found their sex an advantage. Women were viewed as less corrupt than men.

The electorate has become less prejudiced, but some power brokers—political parties, organized groups, big contributors—continue to view women candidates with sexist eyes. They still see women as losers. A woman may run for a "woman's office," such as secretary of state in Connecticut, but she should not get uppity and run for a "man's office."

In the history of the United States, only 11 women have served in the U.S. Senate. Few served a full term and nearly every one was appointed because of her husband's death.

Five women candidates for the Senate were defeated in 1976. One hundred men sit in the Senate today. There are no women senators, which apparently makes it a man's office. That is what Pennsylvania State Senator Jeanette Reidman discovered when she sought the Democratic nomination that year.

> I thought it was time we elected a woman senator, and I thought a large industrial state should be ready for one. I had served in the legislature for twenty years and my name is on three hundred pieces of legislation. Yet the chairman of my own party told me that Pennsylvania was not ready for a woman senator.
>
> One day an emissary of my opponent came to my office and asked me to pull out of the race. He promised that if I withdrew, I would be guaranteed the nomination for state treasurer, a job previously held by women. He said to me, 'That is a woman's job.' I said I would not be part of any deal and that what he said was an insult to women.
>
> When I asked my opponent to debate me, he said, 'How can you debate a grandmother?' I was called a nice Jewish mother. No one called my opponent a nice Irish father. The *Philadelphia Bulletin* grilled me for three hours on the issues and then wrote a story that described my clothes and haircut and minimally discussed my positions.

The attitudes of party leaders have not changed substantially since 1958, when Gloria Schaffer, a Democrat, first placed herself on the auction block. (Schaffer won her party's nomination for the U.S. Senate in 1976 but lost against incumbent Senator Lowell Weicker in the general election.) Party leaders continue to foist women on the electorate when they believe a race is unwinnable. The party asked Gloria to run for the state senate in 1958 because no male candidate would touch the race. Gloria was 27 years old, the mother of two children, and had run for the legislature two years before and lost.

> If the party leaders thought I could win they never would have nominated me. It was a Republican district and it was con-

sidered bad manners to run. On election night, there must have
been dozens of men who thought of suicide—any one of them
could have had the nomination instead of me. I won because
I worked hard and because there was a landslide for Democratic
Governor Abraham Ribicoff. Once I had won, I had a foothold.
I won five more times.

Even with victories behind you, as a woman you must fight
for your party's nomination.

Ella Grasso had been a winner for 20 years. She had served in
the state legislature, as secretary of state of Connecticut, and in
Congress. But when she sought the nomination for governor, she
had to prove she would win before the leaders would consider
her. Grasso was undaunted. She lined up the votes to guarantee
her the nomination. But even then, not until she beat her opponent in his own hometown primary did the party leaders urge
him to accept the lieutenant governor's slot and concede the
nomination to her. After her election, Grasso admitted having
considered running for governor for many years but never be-
lieving it possible. "Women were not candidates," she said.

Mary Anne Krupsak, then a New York state senator, also had
to fight the party bosses to get her name on the primary ballot.
She was running for lieutenant governor of New York, another office never before held by a woman. At first, she was dis-
missed as a potential liability to the state ticket. But in the
end there was more enthusiasm for her candidacy than the
governor's.

Politics is a rough game, and the traditional players want to
hold on to their control. Their power comes from the candidates they choose and get elected. Women have never been part
of the "club," so party leaders do not trust them.

When the time arrived for the party to nominate its candidate for secretary of state in 1970, the Connecticut bosses
dumped Gloria Schaffer. The office was reserved for a woman
and Gloria was the only woman in the party with statewide
visibility; it "belonged" to her. But apparently the leadership
did not like Gloria's independence. They chose a woman who

**Connecticut Secretary of State Gloria Schaffer (left)
with Governor Ella Grasso following their nomination
by the 1974 Democratic State Convention.**

was a political unknown. Gloria fought the party leadership and won. She threatened them with a primary battle and they nominated her.

> I decided to fight the leadership of my party, which I was loath to do. The party is strong and few have cracked it. It was a lesson for me. It taught me that if you think you are right, you should stand up and fight. It was terribly painful. Ella was the only person who defied the general party order, at first. But it helped me get elected. The voters said, "Anyone who can stand up and fight, I am going to be for her."

You do not always need party support. Some local elections are nonpartisan; in some areas, the party has no clout. But if you are running for a statewide office or for Congress, the party has tremendous influence. That influence translates into contributions from the big givers—business, the unions, organized groups. Without it, you have a much tougher time.

Campaigns cost money. Money buys public-opinion polls to analyze where you stand, television time, direct-mail solicitations to raise more money, and skilled workers. Raising money is the biggest problem women candidates face.

Jeanette Reidman of Pennsylvania is convinced she would have won the Senate race if she had had as much money as her opponent. He outspent her three to one and won two to one. "Media is the name of the game in a big state. I campaigned at factory gates every morning. But I couldn't reach everybody. Fund raising was difficult. If I had had more money, my staff would have been better. Volunteers worked passionately for me, but I needed to purchase skills."

Because Maya Miller was considered an underdog when she ran for the U.S. Senate in Nevada, the established groups such as teachers, unions, and state employees endorsed her opponent at the campaign's outset. Maya's campaign caught fire midway, but that was too late. "These endorsements are self-fulfilling," she says. Although the national party is supposed to keep hands off during a primary, they gave money to her opponent. That sent union money into his campaign, too. What shocked

Maya more were the liberal groups that gave him money. She had fought for their causes for years.

Women candidates are still outsiders, but there has been a big change. They are helping one another become candidates and win elections. They are creating their own networks to fill the gap that exists because women are excluded from the normal political routes.

Maya discovered quickly that she could never raise enough money in conservative Nevada to wage a campaign. She had to try something different. Besides traveling out of state to raise money at various events, Maya launched a direct-mail campaign asking for contributions from liberals and women around the country. Her pitch was the importance of having a woman in the Senate. She was successful in raising substantial funds, and to help other women candidates do the same thing, she created the Women's Campaign Fund.

At a press conference the fund held for four female Senate candidates in 1976, the candidates said their biggest problem was raising money. The only national group to give them money was the Women's Campaign Fund.

Even raising money from private people is more difficult for women. Men do not take women's candidacies seriously. When they give to a woman candidate, they give less. Women have not had the money to give, nor are women accustomed to giving large sums to political campaigns. That has always been the man's prerogative.

The Women's Campaign Fund proved in 1976 that women will give to women candidates. Executive Director Carol Randles says that 92 percent of the contributions came from women. That was a year when campaign funds were difficult to come by for anyone.

That same year the National Women's Political Caucus provided assistance to women candidates of both parties. The Women's Education Fund, run by Betsey Wright, saw signs that women were developing their own local political networks. Skills learned working in men's campaigns were being turned over to other women. "I am greatly encouraged by what I see," says Betsey. "The 1976 campaigns are far more sophisticated than they were two years ago. Women still face the same obstacles, but they have learned how to deal with them."

According to Betsey, women can overcome a lack of money with "time and organization." A woman candidate must begin early. She has to build a base of support or a network of supporters. They must organize to the hilt and put all kinds of campaigning skills to good use.

Many women build their base from their connections within the League of Women Voters or the PTA. The Women's Political Caucus has local chapters which can also launch a candidacy. As you campaign, your base grows. You continue building on it as you run for reelection and higher office.

Elaine Noble did not have to create a base. She was urged to run by her neighbors in Boston's Fenway community. Elaine had been taking their battles to an indifferent city government and they knew she would fight for them. From among those residents came the workers for Elaine's campaign. Elaine turned her campaign office into a community center after she won, so she could train other women to run for office.

Maryland State Senator Rosalie Abrams discovered she had a natural base when she first ran for the state legislature. Her father, who had died 20 years before, owned a bakery in their Jewish neighborhood in Baltimore. People remembered him and supported her because of the family tie. That first campaign was organized from Rosalie's kitchen with her sister, mother, and maid mailing out literature to everyone they knew. After her election, Rosalie formed her own organization from that base, which has also seen her through two subsequent campaigns.

> You learn in politics that you are never secure. Your friends take it for granted that you will be reelected and they do not help much. Your enemies organize to get rid of you. I keep my organization active so that when I run I do not have to start from scratch. We support other candidates and organize campaigns for them. That way, when it is my turn, they are ready to work for me.

Elaine Noble campaigns in the streets of Boston in 1974.

Women candidates are discovering that their greatest asset is themselves. It used to be that you had to be married and have grown children before you could venture into politics. Today, younger women are running and winning. These women may be single, divorced, married with young children, or married with no children. While they do not campaign solely on the issue of women's equality, they are not afraid to speak for women.

Women candidates have a natural advantage of standing out in a field of men. Women look better on television because they look different. Because they are outsiders, the voters see women as more honest and committed to public service than men.

Pat Schroeder ran for Congress in 1972 because she offered something new. Pat's campaign poster rejected the traditional smiling candidate with the happy-family image. Instead, she used her face with the words, "This radical troublemaker is out to get something from you—hope."

"To beat the incumbent, we needed a different kind of candidate. The women's movement was gaining momentum. It seemed that I would have a better chance than a young male."

Barbara Mikulski was elected to the Baltimore City Council twice, ran for the U.S. Senate and was defeated, and won her congressional seat in 1976.

"You do not hire a public relations firm to tell you what you ought to be. If you are true to yourself and to your constituency, people will vote for you. The more you get in touch with yourself and project your views, your philosophy, your style, the more effective you become."

Elaine Noble, the first avowed homosexual elected to a state office, did not fudge about who she is.

People warned me against stating that I am a homosexual but I thought it was necessary. That still doesn't make me a one-issue person, however. I have opinions on everything. Senior citizens elected me. They know I go out on a limb for them. I am reclaiming a piece of dignity for people who can't stand up there themselves.

As few officeholders as there are who are *women,* only 4 percent of all *women* officeholders are *black.* But those are highly respected politicians. Yvonne Burke, congresswoman from California, is an attorney, who earlier served in the California legislature. A civil rights activist since the 1950s, Burke gained national prominence as co-chairman of the 1972 Democratic National Convention. Congresswoman Barbara Jordan, an attorney who served in the Texas legislature, is mentioned as a potential presidential or vice-presidential candidate. Jordan, an eloquent speaker, gave such an impressive performance on the House Judiciary Committee during its historic impeachment hearings, that she personally advanced the cause of women in politics.

Doris Bunte, assistant majority leader of the Massachusetts house of representatives, gained a statewide reputation as a forceful leader when she took Boston Mayor Kevin White to court. White appointed Bunte to run the city housing authority and fired her after she fired one of his patronage appointees. "He thought the little black lady from Roxbury would pack up and go away, but I am not made that way," she says. "After the trial, which I won, I recognized that my salability as a politician was high. I fought City Hall and I won. People knew I would fight for them."

Aside from launching a campaign early and developing a sophisticated organization, the most important decision a candidate must make is choosing a campaign manager. You must trust the person who is directing your campaign. Your campaign reflects the person you wish to get across to the electorate— you. Your campaign manager must be sensitive to who you are.

Not only did Maya Miller hire a campaign manager from out of state, she chose a man. That caused occasional problems, but Maya had no regrets. "I needed a professional. I was in the campaign to win. We could train women managers for tomorrow, but I needed someone immediately. I wouldn't be comfortable with an advertising agency type. I needed a person who would be comfortable with my life-style. The great thing about Ken was he understood me. He helped me develop my issues. But they were my issues. I could be myself."

Representative Yvonne Burke speaks to a 1976 meeting of the Caucus of Black Democrats.

Being a candidate is probably the most grueling and at the same time exhilarating experience imaginable. Your time is not your own. You must worry about what you wear, what you say, where you are, at every given moment. Your life is totally controlled. If you have a good campaign manager, you won't plan a minute of your time. It will be planned for you. You campaign from early morning to late at night. The best training for a candidate is working in campaigns. Some candidates relish campaigns, others endure them.

"To run for office, you need stamina," says Barbara Mikulski, a rousing speechmaker and dynamic campaigner. "It is never a nine-to-five routine. You are on your feet a lot. You may begin at plant gates at six A.M. and go until eleven or twelve at night. When I ran for city council, I walked six miles a day up and down stairs. You also must be a good listener. People have their own ideas and they want to bring them to your attention. You cannot talk at them. You have to be able to talk *with* them."

Asking people to vote for her is still difficult for Connecticut's Gloria Schaffer, even 18 years after her first winning campaign. Congresswoman Yvonne Burke has learned to put up with humiliating questions. Her colleague Pat Schroeder enjoyed her first campaign, but the second one—with abortion and busing the outstanding controversial campaign issues—was depressing.

> We had real crazies. They spit on me and screamed "nigger lover." They want you to fight back because then they have made the front page. You have blown your cool and everyone can say, "See, a woman is emotional." Campaigning is fun when you can discuss the issues. I like people and that is what campaigning is about. But if the crazy people are around, they scare off the good people.

You need a thick skin, but sometimes you find that you are tougher than you thought. Maya Miller never liked criticism. Yet she enjoyed facing a hostile audience and winning them over. To many Nevada voters, Maya Miller is a far out liberal who supports such "causes" as the environment and women's liberation.

> I appeared before a group of Mormon women and miners. There were anti-ERA signs all over. They introduced me as an

State Senator Carol Bellamy, during her successful 1977 campaign for New York City council president.

"environmentalist," and I knew that was a dirty word to them. But after I spoke, an old miner stood up and said, "We have had senators come through here before but they never answered our questions. Mrs. Miller answered our questions and I think she would make a good senator." You have to feel pleased after an evening like that.

A good campaigner cannot shy away from combat. When a man runs against a woman, he sometimes feels he cannot attack her straight on. So he uses subtle tactics. Lila Cockrell's opponent for mayor of San Antonio ran on the slogan, "May the best man win." Nancy Hayward faced an opponent for commissioner of Lane County, Oregon, whose slogan was "A man for all reasons."

In her 22 years of public service, Governor Ella Grasso has never shied away from an attack. She is a warm, charming woman, but in a campaign Grasso is a tiger. In her race for governor, she took advantage of the Republican incumbent's record to attack her opponent. She took on the state's three power companies and the public utility commission (PUC). To catch the PUC chairman off guard, Grasso presented him with a report disclosing that Connecticut's homeowners were overcharged $19 million in fuel-adjustment costs in three years—with television cameras close behind. According to a *Washington Post* account, "When a commission aide cautiously asked whether the state officials could cross-examine the writers of the report, Mrs. Grasso replied, 'My dear, I would hope you would feel it is not cross-examining, but sharing information. As a matter of fact, most of this information came from your own files.' She then turned on her heels, and left with as much authority as when she entered."

Congresswoman Yvonne Burke has summed up the issue of what it takes to be an effective campaigner:

"The nature of politics is a fight. You need to be thick-skinned and enjoy pressure. You cannot be shattered if you lose a campaign or a fight in Congress. You have to learn to live with conflict."

9

Women in Office

No matter what office you hold—a seat on the city council or in Congress, whether you are the mayor of a large city or a county commissioner—you will find it demanding, frustrating, and rewarding.

It is easier to change things when you are in on the decision making. To introduce a bill and vote on it, to set a state's priorities and budget, to order a change in policy are all more direct than hammering away from the outside. But moving from the role of outsider to officeholder means assuming more responsibility.

"What freaked me out about running for office," confides Massachusetts Representative Elaine Noble, "was that I had to come up with answers. It is much easier to complain about what is wrong than to do something about it. The 'system' is just a bunch of people making decisions. But you can't change things if you are not on the inside. That means you must be responsible to thousands of people. It means you must put yourself on the line. Unfortunately, most people don't want to give up the time or take the cut in salary. They say they have better things to do."

In addition to those reasons for hesitation, social conditioning has prevented many women from taking that step. Many of those who have are activists motivated by dissatisfaction with the way government was functioning.

"Once I took the plunge, I realized how compatible politics is for me," says Oregon Representative Nancie Fadaley, a minister's daughter. "There is a similarity between my life in the parsonage and my life in politics. I could get involved in the PTA and try to improve schools. But if I really want to do something about my children's school, I do something about state funding. I can get things done as a member of the legislature."

Some temperaments are better suited to one office than another. The chief executive of a state or city has thousands of employees to worry about. Sometimes it takes prodding to keep the wheels of government moving. And in times of crisis, the top person takes the heat. The legislature may pass a law providing for open mental hospitals, but if a patient runs away, the governor gets blamed because a state employee did not keep a close eye on the patient.

A governor has tremendous power. She is responsible for making up the state's budget. She will set priorities and submit them to the legislature, which has the authority to allocate funds. The governor can veto legislation.

"A member of Congress has power without responsibility," says Governor Ella Grasso's chief of staff, Nancy Lewinsohn. Lewinsohn was Grasso's administrative assistant in Congress. "A governor has power with great responsibility. It is a much tougher job."

Most elected officials have a honeymoon period for a few months after their election. Governor Grasso's honeymoon ended early. She discovered that her predecessor had left an $80 million deficit. Plans for expanding programs in health care or education had to be tabled. "The cupboard is bare," she said.

Grasso gave up a limousine and a $7,000 pay raise. She began trimming the budget, and thunder shook the statehouse. You cannot talk about laying off thousands of state employees without threats of strikes and screams of "betrayal." Grasso received the most stinging criticism of her career. When she reached a compromise with union leaders, she faced a recalcitrant legislature. She won that battle, as one senator put it, "Because she has to live with them all year. We can go home."

Like the governor, the mayor of a city has more demands on her time, gets more mail, and is more open to attack than any one member of the council, the city's legislative body. She is the city's political leader. She was elected by all the citizens. She represents the city with other branches of government and private industry, negotiates with city employees, presides at council meetings. She is the eyes and ears of the community.

"It is a much tougher job than I thought," says Mayor Janet Gray Hayes, who served previously as vice-mayor. "The buck stops here. People come in and try to intimidate you. Someone said, to be a success in politics you have to act like a lady and think like a man. That means if you think something is not right, you stand up to opposition. You need a sense of fairness. I am tougher than I thought."

After nine years on the San Antonio council, Lila Cockrell wanted a stronger leadership role. "If you serve that long and you are that involved, you feel a strong urge to serve at the top. You can influence policy to a much greater extent as mayor."

For Kathryn Kirschbaum, who served two terms as mayor of Davenport, Iowa, city government had special challenges. "You are right there on the firing line. City government is the closest to the people. Making government work has to be the most challenging undertaking there is. To accomplish something of significance, you have to get people together to work for a common interest."

Kirschbaum did not sit on the sidelines. She set up a controversial rehabilitation and development program for the inner city. That necessitated raising taxes, which proved to be political suicide for her and led to her defeat in 1975.

"It took considerable courage to continue. But the redevelopment had to be done. It is political demagoguery to say you can continue services and not raise taxes."

In a city, the elected officials closest to the people are the council members. They represent a district and work to see that the residents receive the city services due them. The council, like any legislative body, makes laws to protect the well-being of citizens, monitors the executive branch, and advocates the needs of constituents. The council also appropriates the money that pays for city services.

Barbara Mikulski was a natural for the Baltimore city council. She grew up in an ethnic working-class neighborhood. Trained as a social worker, Barbara found she could help more people by organizing groups than counseling individuals. In the process of fighting battles for her neighbors, Barbara decided she could be even more effective through politics. In 1971, she ran for the city council. She established herself as a people's advocate and easily won reelection four years later.

> I chose the city council because the city is my love. The council is the government closest to the people and it should govern best. The community activist sees only one side of the story. The role of city government is to provide services and mediate conflicts. There are always conflicting interests. The elected official has to handle them in the fairest way. Conflict has always been mediated to a resolution, but usually on the side of those who *have* power against those who *don't*.

In 1976, Barbara won her race for the U.S. Congress where she believes she will be in a better position to serve her constituents.

> Every problem I face in city government has its roots at the national level. For example, in the council I can make sure that the meals program for senior citizens is more equitably administered, but that doesn't deal with the basic problem of providing an income for senior citizens. Our medical technology keeps people alive longer, but it doesn't provide needed services or dignity. Those are national issues.

County government is famous for its concern about sewers and zoning. In areas where county government is important, that is, where there are no major cities, the county also cares for the health, welfare, and education needs of its citizens. Ann Stockett chose the county council over the state legislature even though the position in the legislature pays more and carries more prestige. In Anne Arundel County, Maryland, Ann believes, the council has a greater effect on the quality of people's lives than the state legislature.

"The council is an underrated job. The legislature is in session ninety days a year. We work year round. They have less time to study issues and make decisions than we do. We have only six members, so my vote has more weight. I love what I do. It's an awesome responsibility but it fascinates me."

It is easier for a legislator to sit back and do nothing than it is for an executive. However, most women in Congress play an activist role. They want to influence the direction of the nation and national priorities. The 1975 voting records of congresswomen showed that they oppose a belligerent foreign policy and extravagant military spending and are more liberal than their party leaders.

One of the best-known and best-loved women to serve in Congress is Bella Abzug. In her two terms, Bella was responsible for legislation ending discrimination against women in credit and pension policies; legislation on privacy, impoundment, mass transportation, minimum wage, child care, and much more. She was one of the first six members to discuss the impeachment of President Richard Nixon on the House floor. She got the Democrats to pass a resolution against President Ford's request for emergency funds for Cambodia and Vietnam, a remarkable feat.

When Bella arrived on Capitol Hill in 1970, she was viewed as a loud-mouthed radical. By 1976, she was one of the most respected and effective members. "You have to understand what happened since I came here," Bella said. "I came out of the peace and women's movements. They thought I was a lunatic. Now those causes are supported by a majority of the people. I was out front. Then everybody else caught up."

A practicing labor lawyer before her election to Congress, Bella practiced the art of negotiation and compromise to get her bills passed. She knew how to horse trade, and even took her name off a bill and gave another member the credit so her bill would be passed.

Bella Abzug, candidate for mayor in the New York City 1977 Democratic primary, meets with voters.

Bella wasn't afraid to risk her congressional seat for a primary battle for the Senate. Of five female contenders in 1976, Bella came closest to victory. She organized the most effective campaign, raised as much money as her male opponents, and came within one percentage point of winning. No one doubts that Bella will continue to be a political force and women's advocate.

"It took four men to defeat me," Bella told a group of heartbroken female supporters. "I can't help but feel a bit glorious in defeat."

Congresswoman Pat Schroeder did an unusual thing when she entered Congress. She fought her way onto a committee that appropriates funds for the military and that had always been a rubber stamp for the Defense Department. Most members choose committees that reflect their legislative interests. Pat chose one where she would be an unwelcome dissenter.

"The Armed Services Committee controls about 40 percent of the national budget. I can talk all I want about human issues, but they have the dollars. No one ever questioned their appropriations before. When they asked for another billion dollars for another nuclear carrier, I asked, 'Why do we need another one? We already have three.' "

Although the military budget has not yet been modified, Pat has inspired a few other committee members to join in her dissent. Now she is pushing for reforms that could open up congressional meetings and significantly affect the power of senior members.

"I think I am having an impact. Some older members have been afraid to challenge unfairness. Now here comes a young girl who did it. It is simply not being afraid to stand up to them and ask them tough questions. It is slow, it is not fun, but it is important."

Whether you are a member of Congress or in a state legislature, it is not easy to have much of an effect. A legislature is a deliberative body. They study, debate, and negotiate before they adopt legislation. It usually takes years to get a bill through.

"You work with four hundred and thirty-four people who

have egos as big as all outdoors," says Pat. "You can't just come in and make things happen. Most people don't understand that. They think that if you don't make things happen, then you really don't care."

To get a controversial bill through, you begin by laying the groundwork. You hold committee hearings, organize groups that favor it, and use the press to sway public opinion. It helps to get the leadership behind you. You might begin with a study commission. In Maryland, women legislators and women's groups got the senate president to head a study commission on rape. The commission came up with a package of bills to substantially reform the rape laws. The bills got through almost intact because the president had influence and used it.

One of Oregon's most effective legislators, Nancie Fadaley, appears to be a natural-born politician. But the skills of politics have to be learned.

There is no limit to the abilities you need in politics. The potential to do things is never ending, but you can't come here and sit around and smile at someone and expect to get things done. You need the respect of your colleagues. If you expect someone to vote with you, you have to give him or her a good reason for it. You have to do your homework. I fight against someone on one bill and work with them on another.

Nancie is amazed at all she has accomplished, including getting major environmental legislation and the Equal Rights Amendment passed in Oregon. As for other women in office, the job is all-consuming. Nancie seems driven, but even so the pace apparently agrees with her.

No, it doesn't. I'm grouchy and tired and I look awful. I have to get up tomorrow and drive back to Salem for a work session. I get so tired, I wonder why I do it. There have been times this session when if I had a choice, I would have stayed home. But I don't feel as if I have a choice. I am chairman of the environment/energy committee and close to the governor. That gives me a great advantage. There's work to be done, and I am fortunate to be in a position to do it.

If you are an activist, your frustrations will be greater. So will the risk of not getting reelected. Voting your conscience means being an independent who does not take orders from the governor or your party. It means being controversial.

"A lot of people get reelected who won't stick their necks out," says Maryland State Senator Rosalie Abrams. "I'm not here to take a computer printout of my constituent's views. I was elected because of my judgment. If you see this as the end-all of your life, you're tempted to do things just to get reelected. That is dangerous. I have to vote what I feel is right. But as soon as you take a position that is new or different, you are right out there and you can get shot at."

Women are making waves even in offices that are more conducive to doing nothing than taking an active role. For example, the lieutenant governor of New York was always a ceremonial position before Mary Anne Krupsak took it over. Mary Anne is candid about working with a governor who was not eager to have an activist, female lieutenant governor. But Mary Anne wouldn't sit still. "I refuse to be silent and sit respectfully behind. The reality of the political world is that being the second-highest elected official in New York State gives me less power than the state party chairman." Mary Anne is servicing people's complaints, streamlining the government agencies, and traveling around the state speaking to groups on women's and other issues.

For an ambitious politician, such a job provides visibility and a chance to build a constituency. Ella Grasso turned the office of secretary of state into a people's lobby. Her successor, Gloria Schaffer, sponsored major campaign and election reform and waged an aggressive voter-registration campaign. "I am the chief elections officer but the office is basically noncontroversial. Besides being good politics, I think there is an inherent responsibility in urging more voter participation."

Another unsuccessful U.S. Senate candidate in 1976, Arizona's superintendent of public instruction, Carolyn Warner, transformed that office from a do-nothing position into a vehicle for major reform of the state's education system. It took working 20 hours a day, but she tripled the budget for bilingual education, improved the reading programs, and saved the taxpayers $2 million by instituting a system of tight, efficient cost controls. A businesswoman without a college degree, Warner received more votes in 1974 than any other candidate for any other state office.

Women face special problems and therefore bring special perspectives to government. Most women in office care more about ending sex discrimination than even the most liberal males. Legislation to correct injustice to women has come about because women introduced it.

Difficulties in getting the Equal Rights Amendment ratified demonstrate the need for more women in state legislatures. While Congress passed the ERA in 1971–72, only 34 states have ratified it. It takes 38 states to ratify a constitutional amendment.

"I became a feminist here in the legislature," says Rosalie Abrams, a trained nurse. "Women understand aspects of life that men have no contact with."

When her bill to permit pregnant women to collect unemployment benefits was killed in committee, Rosalie petitioned it on the floor. "I heard middle-class men say that pregnant women shouldn't work. They must work. If you were laid off and were pregnant, you couldn't collect and you weren't eligible for welfare either. That is forced idleness." She faced a similar battle over a bill giving pregnant women the same hospitalization benefits as for any other illness. "Seventy percent of you guys will have your prostates removed," Rosalie told the Maryland Senate. "Women do not have prostates. Yet you are covered. My bill passed, but now I am struggling to see that it is implemented."

When a women's bill comes up in the Maryland legislature, the men snicker and bandy about. They make dirty remarks. Rosalie has found that if she introduces a women's bill, her other legislation is jeopardized. Often she will ask a sympathetic male to introduce it. On the other hand, Pat Schroeder says congresswomen feel strongly about introducing their own bills.

Women in Congress and the state legislatures have been handicapped by a lack of seniority and committee chairman-

Barbara Mikulski (left) and Gloria Steinem hold a news
conference in 1975 to announce the formation of an alliance
of Democratic women to have a woman nominated as
president or vice-president.

ships. Often, they are overlooked and have to fight for leadership positions. And women legislators often have to work harder than the men. Just as women in professional jobs must prove their capabilities before they are considered competent, women in office face the same difficulties.

Another reason women in office often work harder than their male colleagues is because of the perception of the public that they are more responsive and more willing to listen to constituents' problems. Nancie Fadaley gets twice the number of phone calls that her husband, a state senator, gets. Ann Stockett finds that people, particularly women, come to her with personal problems. Elaine Noble's crowded desk is like a checkout line at a supermarket and her phone is always ringing.

Pat Schroeder, the only congresswoman in the Colorado delegation, gets mail from people all over Colorado and the country. It can be a problem because her staff gets tied up answering mail and doesn't have time to work on legislation. "It is like being a senator," she says. "People think I am there to represent them even though they live in another congressman's district. The problem is that I don't have the staff of a senator."

If there were as many congresswomen as men, Pat wouldn't have this problem. Nor would women in office find it difficult to rise to leadership positions or that women's legislation was regarded any differently than any other piece of legislation. As Rosalie Abrams discovered after entering politics: "It is unbelievably important to elect more women to office."

10

Politics
and Personal Lives

You may be wondering whether a politician can have a personal life. Given the inordinate demands on their time and energy, most politicians confess that their personal lives suffer.

At one time, the traditional roles of wife and mother made it nearly impossible for a woman to consider a political career. Her career was her husband and children. Anything else had to come second.

A male politician, on the other hand, needed a wife and children to get elected. They were as integral to his political image as a shirt and tie. Some politicians' wives have recently made it clear that they are lonely, that they resent raising children by themselves, and that they find their public role demeaning. But no one has ever questioned whether a male politician could combine his career with a family.

Expanded career opportunities for women and a vocal women's movement is forcing us to reexamine the traditional sex roles. Fathers are being called upon to do more than bring home a paycheck. And motherhood is no longer defined by the hours spent at home with the children. Growing numbers of young women do not believe that marriage is essential to their identity. They are marrying out of choice rather than social pressure. Married women are asking themselves whether or not they wish to have children, rather than automatically having them. And couples are beginning to share household responsibilities and childrearing so that a married woman does not have to choose between career and family.

In real life, of course, any changes from the traditional can create upheaval in personal lives. A woman pursuing a full-time career today may wonder about her roles as a female, a wife, and a mother.

And for the new political woman, the dilemmas are heightened. Politics demands more hours and emotional energy than most careers. It sometimes requires moving to the state capital (at least part of the year) or to Washington. It is no wonder that most older political women ventured out after their children were grown. Even then, the family adjustments are great.

"I could never do it without a supportive family," says State Senator Betty Roberts of Connecticut. "My teenage children have learned to prepare the meals." When she reached age 40, Betty had asked herself, "What am I going to do with the rest of my life?" She is now the busiest woman in the Connecticut legislature. But even when meetings end at midnight, Betty drives the 45 miles home.

When Mary Louise Smith moved to Washington to chair the Republican party, her physician husband remained in Iowa. He couldn't uproot his career. She was 60; he was 63. "Sure he minds," she says. "But he is really a remarkably flexible man."

Even feminist-lawyer Bella Abzug delayed running for office until her daughters were grown. But being separated from her husband, Martin, a stockbroker, wasn't easy. "Even though I have always been involved in things, it was the first time we had separate living arrangements. It was depressive. I tried living in an apartment but it was lonely by myself. I stayed in a hotel and didn't relate to it much. I went home weekends."

There were a few political women who defied convention years ago and ran for office when their children were young. But there was usually no question that they had two careers.

Governor Ella Grasso says she would never have gotten into politics if she hadn't lived in an extended family situation. Grasso was 33 when she was elected to the legislature. Her youngest child was 18 months old. The story everyone tells about Grasso, the career mother, is the one about when her daughter Susane had the measles.

Susane was so sick I had to sit by her. But while I was sitting there I wrote a budget message for Governor Ribicoff. Actually, it gave me something to do. Until Susane was better, I wouldn't have left her.

Everybody on Olive Street had been there for a hundred years; my uncle next door, my parents across the street, people all around who knew me before I was born, so I could leave my children. They were secure. And I always got home in time to cook supper, even if I had to kill myself in the process. I felt my husband deserved it. You see, I'm an Italian wife.

Women who have started out in politics more recently are trying to work out a life-style that permits combining a political career with a full personal life. Many of these women started climbing up the political ladder while in their twenties and single.

Today, it is certainly no longer a disgrace to be a single woman. You do not have to suffer under the stereotypes of the old maid or the emasculating female who could not find a man. Some women in politics find being single is an advantage and feel fulfilled without a husband and family.

Nor does it seem a disadvantage for women running for office. "People think you are a little strange up to a certain age," says Congresswoman Barbara Mikulski. "At twenty-five, you run into it, but at thirty-nine, they think you are over the hill and it doesn't matter. And the big advantage, of course, is that you have the freedom to make your own time without consulting other people."

The two women elected to Congress in 1976—Barbara Mikulski and Mary Rose Oakar—are both single. For Mary Rose, a woman in her mid-thirties, community involvement in the Cleveland neighborhood where she was born sparked a political career. While Barbara was trained as a social worker, Mary Rose is a teacher.

Cathy Riley was elected to the Maryland legislature when

she was 27. She had less time for social life, but found being unmarried was beneficial to her job. "My life is exciting and I do not think about marrying now. I can go out and have a beer after a session and talk about what has happened. I don't feel left out of anything."

Ann Lewis, a mother with three children, whose political career flowered after her divorce, says politics works on a time schedule that makes it difficult to be considerate of other people.

> If you want to be in a campaign and stick around when the decisions are made, you have to be free to go out and have a beer at midnight. That is hard on a person's private life. I could have done it married and I did, but I know it added tension. It means saying to your family, "This is important to me and I may not see you for a while."

While her three daughters were at home, Ann devoted whatever spare time she had to being with them. "They rejuvenate me," she says. "I think women have the advantage of moving from one role to another quite naturally. My children understand what I do and why and I am lucky they are bright and healthy and happy."

Politics is a social profession. You work long hours and you are intensely involved in what you are doing. You are surrounded by men but many women find it difficult to form lasting relationships in this atmosphere.

"In politics more than any other field you have a lot of mobility. There is a lot of activity with men. My priority has been my career. I get enough involvement dating and I haven't missed an intimate relationship," says Jill Schuker, the 29-year-old executive director of the New England Congressional Caucus. "Still, I think I would like to marry and have a family. It would be difficult to keep up this pace, though, and I can't see myself without my career."

Government lobbyist Susan Tannenbaum, like her friend Jill, didn't feel the lack of an exclusive relationship as long as she was in her twenties. Now, she too is reconsidering and is trying to combine politics with a close relationship with one man.

> It is important to have the experience of being a single person on your own. If I had married out of college, I never would have known what I could do. I didn't feel ready for marriage before, and I have no regrets that I'm not married now. But when you are in your thirties you face the decision of having a family or not. I am spending more time on my personal relationship now, trying to resolve it one way or the other.

Most people want to have an intimate relationship. While men seem more accustomed to separating the emotional and professional sides of their lives, and often give up the emotional to pursue the professional, women are more sensitive to their emotional selves. The way to express your emotional self is through a loving relationship with a man, but to balance an intimate relationship with a career takes work and the cooperation of the man.

Twenty-nine-year-old Shelley Fidler discovered it was possible to live with a man and be absorbed in a job on Capitol Hill and not have either commitment suffer. That required a conscious decision to set priorities. Because her early marriage failed, she is more intent on making her present relationship work. Because the man she lives with is also involved in politics, he understands the demands. Shelley has decided that her political career is not the most important part of her life:

> When I am at work, I love it and work as hard as I can. When something is particularly important, I give the extra hours to my job. But I know my job is not my life. I think many people in politics become their job. That is dreadful because when they lose their job they are nothing. As you become older, you decide there are choices to be made about what is important.

Having a family, of course, complicates lives far more. Congresswomen who have husbands and children say the decision making that went into working out a compatible life-style was painful. But somehow they survived it, and now, are balancing the two.

When Margaret Heckler, an attorney, was elected to Congress, it was not possible for her husband, John, to move his investment business to Washington. So Margaret brought her children to Washington and set up a household by herself.

"It was the most difficult period in my whole life," she says. "We had always had two careers, but suddenly all the responsibilities converged on me in almost crisis proportions." Today, she says their lives are under control. There is frequent travel back and forth from Massachusetts to Washington. "It is really very simple. Early on, we set down two principles. We always had first-rate housekeepers and we decided that the important issue in raising the children would be the quality and regularity—not the quantity—of time that we spent together.

Women officeholders whether in Washington or their hometowns stress that without the cooperation of their husbands they could never manage. A man has to be willing to loosen up his professional commitments and be more available to be a father.

Pat Schroeder's husband is her most devoted supporter. He is also an attorney and gave up a better job in Colorado for a position in Washington that permitted him a flexible schedule. Pat's greatest obstacle wasn't her husband or her children, but her own attitudes about her role. She had been used to working part-time and spending more time at home. When she came to Washington there was no question that she would have to hire a housekeeper, but even that step was very difficult for her.

> You can be well educated, you can be objective, and you can say, "if a man can have a career and a family why can't a woman?" But it is hard to overcome those twenty-odd years of conditioning that says you can't do it. I ran [for office] not thinking I would win, and I won. The amazing thing is that you find that your worst fears, about failing as a wife and mother, are simply unfounded.

Pat says the time she spends with her children is quality time. She believes that the freedom from housekeeping tasks makes

Representative Pat Schroeder, during a 1973 protest by working mothers against cutbacks in federally funded day care centers, brought her daughter to the office.

it easier for parent and children to enjoy one another. "We are friends. I believe I am better at nurturing the children because I am not bothered trying to do the other things."

Combining politics and a family life isn't easy but it can be done. No question, it requires sacrifice by both partners and a commitment to making the marriage work. Yvonne Burke is a living example of how a woman can combine the two successfully. Her first marriage ended in divorce and Yvonne remarried just after her election to Congress. During that term, she gave birth to her first child. She was 39.

"Both people have to be willing to make adjustments. But the day is over when women have to choose between a family and a career because they are women."

11

Conclusion

Women have a special part to play in political life today. They can bring a new perspective to government. Whether you are elected to office or work for an officeholder, whether you lobby or organize, you can make government more personal, more concerned about human needs and values, and more honest.

The challenges of a political career are limitless. You can help bring about women's equality. You can make our society more just. You will make decisions that affect the survival of our planet.

The women who have chosen politics as a career are making a difference, but they need more women with them and they have made your entry into the political world easier. If you see your life as an opportunity to change our society for the better, you should consider making politics your career.

Bibliography

ABZUG, BELLA S. *Bella! Ms. Abzug Goes to Washington.* New York: Saturday Review Press, 1972.

CHAMBERLIN, HOPE. *A Minority of Members: Women in the U.S. Congress.* New York: Praeger, 1973.

COOLIDGE, OLIVIA. *Women's Rights: The Suffrage Movement in America 1848–1920.* New York: E. P. Dutton & Co., 1966.

"Forty Years of a Great Idea." *A History of the League of Women Voters.* The League of Women Voters, 1730 M St., N.W., Washington, D.C. 20036

GRUBERG, MARTIN. *Women in American Politics: An Assessment and Sourcebook.* Oshkosh, Wis.: Academia Press, 1968.

JOHNSON, MARILYN, and KATHY STANWICK. "Profile of Women Holding Office." In *Women in Public Office: A Biographical Directory and Statistical Analysis.* New York: R. R. Bowker Company, 1976.

KIRKPATRICK, JEANE J. *Political Woman.* New York: Basic Books, Inc., 1974.

LAMSON, PEGGY. *Few Are Chosen: American Women in Political Life Today.* Boston: Houghton Mifflin Company, 1968.

MACPHERSON, MYRA. *The Power Lovers: An Intimate Look at Politics and Marriage.* New York: G. P. Putnam's Sons, 1975.

Sexism in the Senate, A Study of Employment on Capitol Hill. The Women's Political Caucus of Capitol Hill, 1975.

SIDDON, SALLY GOODYEAR. *Consider Yourself for Public Office.* National Federation of Republican Women, 310 First St., S.E., Washington, D.C. 20003 (Available for $1.00).

TOLCHIN, SUSAN and MARTIN. *Clout: Womanpower and Politics.* New York: Coward, McCann and Geoghegan, 1974.

The Washington Lobby, Congressional Quarterly Publication, 1414 22nd St., N.W., Washington, D.C.

Appendix

Courses and Information on Women in Politics

Center for the American Woman and Politics, Eagleton Institute of Politics of Rutgers University, New Brunswick, New Jersey. Director: Ruth Mandel. Research and statistical information. Projects, workshops, research grants are available.

National Women's Education Fund, 1532 16th St. N.W., Washington, D.C. 20036. Director: Betsey Wright. Campaign workshops. Campaign workbook (to be published).

The Washington Institute for Women in Politics, Mount Vernon College, 2100 Foxhall Rd., N.W., Washington, D.C. 20007. Director: Dr. Susan Tolchin. Workshops, courses and degree program with internship component.

Political Parties

Democratic National Committee, Women's Division, 1625 Massachusettes Avenue, N.W., Washington, D.C. 20036. Campaign materials and information.

National Federation of Republican Women, 310 First St., S.E., Washington, D.C. 20003.

National Women's Political Caucus, 1921 Pennsylvania Ave., N.W., Washington, D.C. 20006. Membership organization. Provides assistance to candidates. Feminist task forces organize women at Democratic and Republican conventions.

Publications

Women's Agenda. The Women's Action Alliance, 370 Lexington Ave., Room 600, New York, N.Y. 10017. Published monthly. $10 per year.

Women's Political Times, published quarterly by the National Women's Political Caucus, 1921 Pennsylvania Ave., N.W., Washington, D.C. 20006. Available along with a newsletter to members. $15.00 membership fee.

Fund raising

Women's Campaign Fund, 122 Maryland Avenue, N.E., Washington, D.C. 20002. Provides campaign funds for women candidates.

Washington Center for Learning Alternatives, 1705 DeSalle St., N.W., Washington, D.C. 20036, (202–659–8510). Provides comprehensive internships in Washington, D.C., for undergraduate and graduate students.

The National Center for Public Internship Programs publishes three directories: *The Directory of Washington Internships for Undergraduates and Graduate Students; Directory of Public Service Internships for Graduate, Post-Graduate, and Mid-Career Professionals;* and the *Directory of Undergraduate Internship Programs* which focuses on programs around the country. Each directory costs $6.00 and can be purchased by writing NCPSIP, 1735 Eye Street, N.W., Suite 601, Washington, D.C. 20006.

Democratic and Republican National Committees have internships. Write them directly at the addresses given for "Political Parties," above.

National Women's Political Caucus, Women's Campaign Fund, National Women's Education Fund use interns. Write them directly.

White House Fellowships are available through the President's Commission on White House Fellowships, Washington, D.C. 20415. Available to "individuals who have been outstanding in their professional fields."

White House interns. Apply to the White House Director of Youth Affairs, Old Executive Office Building, N.W., Washington, D.C.

Publications

"Summer Internships in Washington, D.C." Mademoiselle Magazine, 350 Madison Ave., New York, New York, 10007. Copyright 1975. A reprint is $0.50.

Directory of Public Service Internships; Directory of Public Service Internships for Graduate, Post-Graduate, and Mid-Career Professionals. National Center for Public Service Internships, 1735 Eye St., N.W., Suite 601, Washington, D.C. 20006, (202–331–1516).

Lobbying Organizations (information on women's issues before Congress, etc.)

National Organization For Women, 425 13th St., N.W., Suite 1001, Washington, D.C. 20004, (202–347–2279).

Congressional Clearinghouse on Women's Rights, 722 House Annex Building, Washington, D.C. 20515, (202–225–2947). Ms. Carol Forbes, Director. CCOWR provides a weekly information sheet and newsletter.

Women's Lobby, 1345 G. St., S.E., Washington, D.C. 20002, (202–547–0044).

Index